PRAYERS T

for Leaders

Scriptural Prayers for Effective Leadership In Business, Ministry, and Public Service

James 5:16

by
Germaine Copeland
and
Lane M. Holland

And this is the confidence that we have in him, that, if we ask any thing according to his will, he heareth us: and if we know that he hears us, whatsoever we ask, we know that we have the petitions that we desired of him.

1 John 5:14,15

Harrison House
Tulsa, Oklahoma

12 11 10 09 08   10 9 8 7 6 5 4 3 2 1

Prayers That Avail Much® for Leaders:
Scriptural Prayers for Effective Leadership in Business, Ministry, and Public Service
ISBN 13: 978-1-57794-945-9
ISBN 10: 1-57794-945-5
Copyright © 2008 by Germaine Copeland
Germaine Copeland, President
Word Ministries, Inc.
38 Sloan Street
Roswell, Georgia 30075
www.prayers.org

Published by Harrison House, Inc.
P.O. Box 35035
Tulsa, Oklahoma 74153
www.harrisonhouse.com

ACKNOWLEDGEMENTS

Thank you, Lane Holland, for working alongside me so diligently on this book. I couldn't have done it without your prayers, your knowledge, and so much more that you did to make *Prayers That Avail Much® for Leaders* possible.

Thank you, Marion Jernigan, for your years of service as my personal assistant. After receiving an e-mail requesting that I write a prayer book for politicians, you believed that the idea was a God idea and persevered until I caught the vision. Thank you for giving me Pastor Johnny Enlow's book, *The Seven Mountain Prophecy,* which was the inspiration for adding the prayers of intercession.

A heartfelt thank you to each team member of the Word Ministries prayer group who has contributed to this work praying for Lane and me as they eagerly awaited the publication of this book.

Lane and I also want to thank a group of women known as "The Generals" who prayed and gave suggestions and pointed us in the direction of resources for this book.

Thank you, Cindy Jacobs, president of Generals International and Deborah Company, for encouraging me to include prayers of intercession for the seven major societal issues. We are the Deborahs who "pray, change nations, and buy shoes."

Many thanks to my husband, Everette, for keeping the office and our household organized and running smoothly during the many months I worked on the completion of this book.

We especially want to thank Pastors Joe and Linda Wingo of Emmanuel Praise Church, home of Angel Food Ministries, for their support. And a special thanks to the I.T. staff that kept our computers and printers in top condition!

TABLE OF CONTENTS

Section II: Personal Prayers for Government Leaders

Section III: Personal Prayers for Spiritual Leaders

Appendices

"If my people, who are called by my name, will humble themselves and pray and seek my face and turn from their wicked ways, then will I hear from heaven and will forgive their sin and will heal their land."

2 CHRONICLES 7:14

Preface

You have in your hand a book of tried and proven prayers that will build your faith and keep you strong and confident as you conduct business according to godly principles and precepts. When you humble yourself before God and seek Him, repent for your mistakes (sins), and refuse to sit in the seat of the scornful and ungodly, you will discover solutions to complex challenges even when others have exhausted their resources. Your wise decisions will bring change to hopeless situations, and your influence will increase. Finding favor with God and with man, you will walk in understanding and give favor to others.

Several years ago I wrote *Prayers That Avail Much for the Workplace*, published by Harrison House in Tulsa, Oklahoma. This book has been widely received by "marketplace ministers." They do not leave their "religion" neatly tucked away to be brought out on Sundays or until the next church service. They are in the world Monday through Friday depending on the guidance of God who is the great "I Am." He is always present in every transaction, in every relationship.

God hears you when you pray according to His will and His Word. Your leadership skills become more prominent, and you become a stronger leader in government, ministry, and/or business when you give Jesus preeminence and take time to converse with the Creator of all things. Make Him the center of all you do.

Webster's Revised Unabridged Dictionary defines a leader as "the head or leader of any body of men; a commander, as of an army; a head man, as of a tribe, clan, or family; a person in authority who directs the work of others; the principal actor or agent."[1] The male or female leader's sphere of influence is far-reaching and helps to form society's way of thinking and culture—and that is a tremendous challenge.

We are praying for leaders who will have an understanding of God's military operation. This operation is not taking place within the church but in the marketplace. We have sat by and allowed the enemy to build mountains of influence in various areas of society, turning people away from God's purpose and plan, and now we have to take these mountains for the kingdom of God. In this way we can bring reformation to society.

You are one of the leaders who will "go and make disciples of all the nations." Invite the Holy Spirit to be your constant companion, that you might be an effective witness to the ends (the very bounds) of the earth[2]. This will not be done only inside the four walls of the church.

God gives prayer strategy and equips His "ministers of a new covenant" to move in and out of the world systems, the mountains of media, government, business, religion, family, education, and entertainment. He intends for the body of Christ to take charge of these societal structures or "gates of society" for the purpose of bringing reformation to our world.

---

[1] Internet: *Webster's Revised Unabridged Dictionary,* © 1996, 1998 MICRA, Inc.

[2] Acts 1:8 AMP

God knew you before the foundation of the world, and He included you in His master plan. You are a leader who has a sacred appointment to function effectively in your area of influence. Just like in the beginning, you are to use all the gifts and abilities God gave you to fulfill the same commandment that He gave to Adam and Eve. He blessed them and said, "Be fruitful, multiply, and fill the earth, and subdue it [using all its vast resources in the service of God and man]; and have dominion over the fish of the sea, the birds of the air, and over every living creature that moves upon the earth[3].

"No authority exists except from God [by His permission, His sanction], and those that exist do so by God's appointment."[4] You have been appointed by the Leader for the good of the people and to the glory of God! May God's will be done on earth even as it is in heaven!

Each generation looks for leaders, statesmen and stateswomen who will follow after righteousness (do what is right and just), and who will bring about reformation in the nation. Effective leaders take responsibility for their own actions, repairing and improving the spiritual, social, intellectual, and emotional climate of a people. The voice of righteous leaders is heard as they serve God in the marketplaces. God-fearing leaders are examples to the present generation and leave a legacy of greatness for the next generation to build upon.

[3] Genesis 1:28 AMP

[4] Romans 13:1

"God, in this hour, is raising up reformers to bring change into the political and social areas of our culture. Voices are being heard both in the church and society. Some of the voices of reformation are calling out for change that is contrary to our Christian foundations. God must have His true reformers in the Church who will read the signs that the Lord is sending and become the voice of the Lord in the earth!"[5]

What is the purpose of writing a book of prayers for leaders? Prayer is a form of communication, a way to talk with the God who appointed you. You face many complex, intricate situations, and people look to you for answers. Prayer positions you to receive godly wisdom that will give you the tools to probe and understand mysteries.

The prayer of praise and worship keeps your heart flexible and your mind open to new ideas and witty inventions that contribute to the good of society. It enables you to give guidance and assurance for the good and welfare of the people. Prayer attunes your ear to hear the voice of God. Sir Thomas Buxton wrote, "You know the value of prayer; it is precious beyond all price. Never, never neglect it."[6]

One of the great leaders of the Old Testament Scriptures was Moses, a man who had an overwhelming call from God to lead a nation out of bondage. He drew near to the presence of God because he recognized his need for divine guidance. Prayer is communication with your God, this awesome

---

[5] Vol. 5, No. 1 of *Culture Reformers,* February 1, 2008, Barbara Wentroble, International Breakthrough Ministries.

[6] *Prayer Devotional Bible,* (Grand Rapids, Michigan: Zondervan, 2004), p. 240.

Presence, who has promised to lead you on a level ground. There is power in prayer, power for every situation and circumstance you face.

Praying scriptural prayers is one proven method for drawing near to His presence. Praying and meditating on scriptural prayers will give you greater knowledge and understanding of righteousness, and you will come into a closer relationship with the Master Leader, the God of the Universe. Understanding righteousness gives you a clear knowledge of justice and right behavior. You will live in this truth: "The foolishness of God is wiser than men, and the weakness of God is stronger than men."[7]

This book of scriptural prayers was written with you in mind. The prayers are for all leaders in government and business, as well as the ecumenical environment. They are written to help you to grow in the knowledge of God and revelation of His great and precious promises. Then, through them you may walk in the divine nature and escape the corruption in the world caused by evil desires.[8]

We have included in this edition statements by men and women who have influenced this nation and the world by their leadership abilities. By including them we are by no means saying they were or are without fault, but they simply exemplify the essence of leadership qualities that we need to remember at this time in our nation.

Germaine Copeland
Lane Holland

---

[7] 1 Corinthians 1:25
[8] 2 Peter 1:2-4

"We have been the recipients of the choicest bounties of heaven, we have been preserved these many years in peace and prosperity; we have grown in number, wealth, and powers as no other nation has ever grown, but we have forgotten God! Intoxicated with unbroken success, we have become too self-sufficient to feel the necessity of redeeming and preserving grace, too proud to pray to the God who made us."

ABRAHAM LINCOLN

Prayer for the Seven Mountains of Society

Taking the knowledge of God out of our society has resulted in many changes. There was a time when a person's word was their bond, when corruption was the exception, children were taught good morals, right was right and wrong was wrong, and we felt safe in our communities. Freedom was not the right to do as you please regardless of who you hurt. Freedom was the right to live truly, speak truly, and deal truly.

This was the world where I grew up, and it was a safe environment. I want an even better world for my grandchildren and future generations—a world where the royal law of love is evident, where we are experiencing the more abundant life—where God's will is done on earth even as it is in heaven.

Have you taken account of the world we live in today? Have you asked yourself why our cities are filled with crime and immorality? Who is controlling our society, molding the minds of our children and society?

What will it take to stop the downward spiral and rebuild our societal structure according to biblical principles and precepts? We are in need of a reformation! Let it begin in the prayer closet, where the Holy Spirit will give you strategies for transforming your workplace, your city, your church, and your nation.

In the beginning God blessed the man and woman and said to them, "Be fruitful, multiply, and fill the earth, and subdue it [using all its vast resources in the service of God and man]; and have dominion over the fish of the sea, the birds of the air, and over every living creature that moves upon the earth."[1] The church is to put on the whole armor of God and be the primary influence in this world where we live.

We are seated in heavenly places in Christ: Far above all principality, and power, and might, and dominion, and every name that is named, not only in this world, but also in that which is to come.[2] Once again, the world is looking for answers, for hope, and we are to be God's instruments of change in the earth.

Where are the spiritual leaders who are equipping believers to go into the entire world for the work of the ministry? Ministry takes place outside the four walls of the church, and God is downloading information, strategies for victory for those who have ears to hear. The marketplace ministers will reverse the downward spiral, where corruption and sin are running rampant and the family structure is being destroyed.

It was in the fall of 2007 that I first heard about the "Seven Mountain Strategy." As I listened to the speaker, Lance Wallnau, I knew that I was to write prayers related to this message. I was amazed to learn that this revelation was given to two men, Loren Cunningham of Youth With a Mission (YWAM) and the now-deceased leader of Campus Crusade, Bill Bright. God revealed to both men that believers

---

[1] Genesis 1:28 AMP

[2] Ephesians 1:20,21, 2:6

are to take the "seven mind-molders of society." If believers can take these mountains we will capture the nation.

As the minister spoke my thinking was radically changed. The world isn't coming to the church; we have to take our message to the world—not only to preach it but to live it in the marketplaces of our nations. God was the "I Am" when Moses freed a nation from slavery, and this same "I Am" wants to be in the center of our everyday, going-to-work life. He is raising up leaders who are kingdom-minded, who are fulfilling the Great Commission to go into all the world and make disciples of all the nations.

Johnny Enlow addresses this wonderful revelation in his book, *The Seven Mountain Prophecy.* Pastor Enlow has identified the seven mountains as:

The Mountain of Media

The Mountain of Government

The Mountain of Education

The Mountain of Economy

The Mountain of Religion

The Mountain of Celebration

The Mountain of Family

In Section V there are prayers of intercession that will prepare the way for leaders to go forth in the power of the Holy Spirit under the banner of love. The world will know that God loves them as we practice the royal law of love in the marketplaces—the societal structures of this world system.

"In the swift rush of great events, we find ourselves groping to know the full sense and meaning of these times in which we live. In our quest of understanding, we beseech God's guidance."

DWIGHT EISENHOWER

Meeting with God

The Holy Spirit will help you understand the present day signs of the times. When you come to a time of prayer and meditation, visualize the God of the universe in the boardroom of heaven where you are seated. At the head of the conference table is the Master Planner and at His right hand is Jesus. The Holy Spirit is beside you as your Divine Helper to give you understanding and help you offer your petitions.

Always take time to worship the Father, to offer Him thanksgiving and acknowledge who He is. Worship at His footstool and approach Him with confidence. Here in His Throne Room you will receive mercy and find grace to help in your time of need.

The prayers in this book are written for your devotional times. Pray your selections aloud in conversational tones. Reading and meditating on the listed Scripture references will help you stay focused and keep your mind on God.

After you have prayed, give the Holy Spirit quality time to make the Word a reality in your heart. Your inner person (spirit-being) will become alive to God's Word, and you will receive the "salvation of your soul" as you renew your thought processes. You will even begin to think like God thinks and talk like He talks during business hours throughout the day.

Jesus prayed and received instruction from the Father. He spoke what the Father gave Him to say and did the things He showed Him to do. He always had a ready answer for those who came to Him, and His words were filled with authority. He did not bring another form of religion, but He came to bring life—a more abundant life.

Research and contemplate the spiritual significance of each verse listed with the prayers. These are by no means the only scriptures on certain subjects, but they are a beginning.

You will not be disappointed because the Father-God rewards those who diligently seek Him. When you pray in secret the Father rewards you openly. What is it that you desire of Him?

These prayers are a guide for you to have a more personal relationship with the Master Leader, the One who prepared the heavens and the earth for mankind. Prayer and the study of His Word transform your mind and lifestyle, and you will become more confident in your leadership ability. Others will witness the transformation in you. You will have a ready answer for those who ask about your success or seek your advice. When you counsel someone with the Word, you will offer spiritual wisdom and encouragement.

Walk in God's counsel and prize His wisdom. People are looking for something on which they can depend. When someone in need comes to you with a problem, you can point them to that portion in God's Word that is the answer. You can walk as an example of an effective, victorious, trust-worthy leader, and others will learn to trust and follow you. You can point them to the One who knows all things, the One who can show them the pathway to success and victory.

Once you begin studying God's Word, determine to be a doer of the Word, ordering your conversation aright. Faith always has a good report. You cannot pray effectively about any situation while thinking and talking negatively about the matter. Until your thoughts and conversation are congruent with the Scriptures, you will find that you are being double-minded, and a double-minded individual receives nothing from God.

In Ephesians 4:29,30 AMP it is written:

> Let no foul or polluting language, nor evil word, nor unwholesome or worthless talk [ever] come out of your mouth; but only such [speech] as is good and beneficial to the spiritual progress of others, as is fitting to the need and the occasion, that it may be a blessing and give grace (God's favor) to those who hear it.

> And do not grieve the Holy Spirit of God, (do not offend, or vex, or sadden Him) by whom you were sealed (marked, branded as God's own, secured) for the day of redemption—of final deliverance through Christ from evil and the consequences of sin.

Reflect on these words and give them time to adjust your perspective and line up your thoughts with God's will. Our Father has much, so very much, to say about that little member, the tongue. Give the devil no opportunity by getting into worry, unforgiveness, wrangling, strife, and criticism. Put a stop to idle and foolish talking. Your words are to be a blessing to others.

Talk the answer not the problem. If you are abiding in Jesus and His Word is abiding in you, the answers are within your being, and the Holy Spirit is your guide. "The plans of the mind belong to man, but the answer of the tongue is from the Lord."[1] When you turn your ear to wisdom and apply your heart to understanding...you will find the knowledge of God. [2] Ask for revealed knowledge of God's Word. The Holy Spirit, your Teacher, will reveal the things that have been freely given to you by God.

[1] Proverbs 16:1 RSV
[2] Proverbs 2:2-4

"Never doubt that a small group of
thoughtful, concerned citizens can change
the world. Indeed it is the only thing that
ever has."

MARGARET MEAD

United, Steadfast Prayer

Jesus revealed the power of united prayer when He said, "Take this most seriously: A yes on earth is yes in heaven; a no on earth is no in heaven. What you say to one another is eternal. I mean this. When two of you get together on anything at all on earth and make a prayer of it, my Father in heaven goes into action. And when two or three of you are together because of me, you can be sure that I'll be there" (Matthew 18:18-20 THE MESSAGE).

United prayer is a mighty weapon that the body of Christ is to employ. Also, consider asking a few people that you know well to pray for you daily or weekly. If Jesus asked three of His disciples to pray for Him, how much more do we need others to pray for and with us?

Encourage your prayer partners to have the faith of God and approach Him boldly, with confidence. Pray according to His will, He will hear you, and you will have what you ask of Him. Do not throw away your confidence. It will be richly rewarded.

Allow your spirits to pray by the Holy Spirit, and walk by faith and not by sight. After you have asked, believe you have received and praise Him for giving you the wise answer, for showing you the way to resolve problems and giving you innovative plans for action.

When your own faith comes under pressure, don't be moved. The more successful you are the more others will seek you out. And get to know those who wish to pray with you. Not everyone is sent from God. There are a few who come with personal agendas, and they are not there to help you fulfill your vision. Beware of wolves in sheep's clothing. Watch and pray. God will give you discernment.

Steer clear of strife! Be of one mind and in one accord. It is the prayer of agreement that assures us of answered prayer. Jesus prayed for His followers to walk together in harmony, united in purpose. In John 17 He prayed, "The goal is for all of them to become one heart and mind—Just as you, Father, are in me and I in you, So they might be one heart and mind with us. Then the world might believe that you, in fact, sent me."

Avoid walking in the counsel of the wicked, standing in the way of sinners, or sitting in the seat of mockers. They will become thorns in your side, and Satan will take advantage of situations to turn you away from righteousness and hinder your God-given goals and purposes. When Satan attempts to challenge you, resist him steadfast in the faith— letting patience have her perfect work. Take the sword of the Spirit and the shield of faith and quench his every fiery dart.

Satan, the enemy of your soul, is now a defeated foe because Jesus conquered him. He is overcome by the blood of the Lamb and the word of your testimony. Fight the good fight of faith. Withstand the adversary and be firm in faith against his onset—rooted, established, strong, and determined. When you know that you have heard from the Father, speak His Word boldly and courageously.

Go into the marketplaces knowing you are called by Jesus to "go out and train everyone you meet, far and near, in this way of life, marking them by baptism in the threefold name: Father, Son, and Holy Spirit. Then instruct them in the practice of all I have commanded you. I'll be with you as you do this, day after day after day, right up to the end of the age."

Love the Lord your God with all your being and come into His presence knowing that you are welcome. As you pray according to His Word, He joyfully hears that you are living and walking in the truth. Rejoice because your prayers are forever in the throne room.

The answers may not come when you want them to, but rest assured that the Father hears and answers prayer. Praise God for His Word and the limitlessness of prayer in the name of Jesus. It belongs to every child of God. Therefore, run with patience the race that is set before you, looking unto Jesus, the author and finisher of your faith. God's Word is able to build you up and give you your rightful inheritance among all God's set-apart ones.

Commit yourself to pray with others, to encourage others to pray for you, and to pray correctly by approaching the throne with your mouth filled with His Word.

Scripture References

Hebrews 11:6   Matthew 6:6

Psalm 1   Proverbs 4:7, 8

Psalm 50:23   Matthew 12:34-37

James 1:6-8   James 3

Ephesians 4:27; 5:4   Galatians 6:10

Proverbs 16:1   Proverbs 2:1-5

John 14:26   1 John 5:14,15

2 Corinthians 5:7   Psalm 1

Numbers 33:55   James 1:4

Ephesians 6:16, 17   Colossians 2:14,15

Revelation 12:11   1 Timothy 6:12

1 Peter 5:9   3 John 4

Revelation 5:8   Hebrews 12:1,2

Acts 20:32   Matthew 28:19,20 THE MESSAGE

"There is no way that Christians, in a private capacity, can do so much to promote the work of God and advance the kingdom of Christ as by prayer."

JONATHAN EDWARDS

The Power of Prayer

The earnest (heart-felt, continued) prayer of a righteous man makes tremendous power available—dynamic in its working. Prayer is fellowshipping with the Father—vital, personal contact with God, who is more than enough. We are to be in constant communion with Him because the eyes of the Lord are upon the righteous—those who are upright and in right standing with God—and His ears are attentive (open) to their prayer.

Prayer is not to be a religious form with no power. It is to be effective and accurate and bring results. God watches over His Word to perform it. Ask God for divine guidance as you approach each day with its new challenges and victories.

Prayer that brings results must be based on God's Word. For the Word that God speaks is alive and full of power—making it active, operative, energizing and effective; it is sharper than any two-edged sword, penetrating to the dividing line of the breath of life (soul) and [the immortal] spirit, and of joints and marrow [that is, of the deepest parts of our nature] exposing and sifting and analyzing and judging the very thoughts and purposes of the heart.

Prayer is this "living" Word in our mouths. We release our faith by speaking faith-filled words; faith is what pleases God. We hold His Word up to Him in prayer, and our Father sees Himself in His Word.

Approaching God

God's Word is our contact with Him. We put Him in remembrance of His Word, placing a demand on His ability in the name of our Lord Jesus. Our faith increases when we remind Him that He supplies our every need according to His riches in glory by Christ Jesus. His Word does not return to Him void—without producing any effect, useless—but it shall accomplish that which He pleases and purposes, and it shall prosper in the thing for which He sent it.

God did not leave us without His thoughts and His ways, for we have His Word—His bond. God instructs us to call Him, and He will answer and show us great and mighty things. Prayer is an exciting adventure.

As you pray in faith the same Holy Spirit who was hovering over the face of the waters in Genesis 1 begins moving to bring about the desired results. The eyes of God run to and fro throughout the whole earth to show Himself strong in behalf of those whose hearts are blameless toward Him.

According to the Word, those who are in Christ are blameless and are in right standing with God as His very own children. He tells us to come boldly to the throne of grace and obtain mercy and find grace to help in time of need—appropriate and well-timed help. Come into His presence with singing and enter His gates with thanksgiving; you are always welcome there.

God Provides Prayer Armor

God has provided a tried-and-true prayer armor for every believer, every member of the body of Christ. We have been instructed to get dressed—to put it on and walk in it, for the weapons of our warfare are not carnal but mighty through God for the pulling down of the strongholds of the enemy (Satan, the god of this world, and all his demonic forces).

In Ephesians 6 we are instructed to take the sword of the Spirit, which is the Word of God, and pray at all times—on every occasion, in every season—in the Spirit, with all [manner of] prayer and entreaty. There are many different kinds of prayer, such as the prayer of thanksgiving and praise, the prayer of dedication, and the prayer of supplication. But all prayer involves a time of fellowship with the Father.

Moses was a leader of a great nation, who knew God and was not afraid to reason with Him on behalf of the people. In First Timothy 2 we are admonished and urged that petitions, prayers, intercessions, and thanksgivings be offered on behalf of all men. Prayer is our responsibility.

Scriptural prayer is one of the major building blocks for success. God desires for His people to be successful, to be filled with a full, deep, and clear knowledge of His will (His Word) and to bear fruit in every good work. We then bring honor and glory to Him. He desires that we know how to pray, for the prayer of the upright is His delight.

Our Father has not left us helpless. Not only has He given us His Word, but also He has given us the Holy Spirit to help our infirmities when we know not how to pray as we ought. Our Father has provided His people with every possible avenue to ensure their complete and total victory in this life in the name of our Lord Jesus.

We pray to the Father, in the name of Jesus, with the help of the Holy Spirit, according to the Word. Using God's Word on purpose, specifically, in prayer is one means of prayer, and it is a most effective and accurate means. Jesus said, "The words (truths) that I have been speaking to you are spirit and life."

God's Word Is the Key to Success

When Jesus faced Satan in the wilderness, He said, "It is written...it is written...it is written." We are to live, be upheld by, and be sustained by every word that proceeds from the mouth of God.

James, by the Spirit, admonishes us that we do not have because we do not ask. We ask and receive not because we ask amiss. We must heed that reprimand now, for we are to become experts in prayer, rightly dividing the Word of Truth. What is our God-given destiny? Prayer will prepare our hearts to do those good works which God predestined (planned beforehand) for us. Scriptural prayer opens our eyes to see the paths which God prepared ahead of time that we should walk in them.

Using the Word in prayer is not taking it out of context, for His Word in us is the key to answered prayer—to prayer that brings results. He is able to do exceedingly abundantly above all we ask or think, according to the power that works in us. The power lies within God's Word.

We apply that Word personally to ourselves and to others—not adding to or taking from it. We apply the Word to the now—to those things, circumstances, and situations facing each of us now.

In the Old Testament Moses and others prayed for the nation of Israel. In the New Testament Paul was very specific and definite in his praying. The first chapters of Ephesians, Philippians, Colossians, and 2 Thessalonians are examples of how Paul prayed for believers. There are numerous others. Search them out. Paul wrote under the inspiration of the Holy Spirit. We can use these Spirit-given prayers today!

In 2 Corinthians 1:11, 2 Corinthians 9:14, and Philippians 1:4, we see examples of how believers prayed one for another—putting others first in their prayer life with joy. Our faith does work by love. We grow spiritually as we reach out to help others—praying for and with them and holding out to them the Word of Life.

You are a spirit being who has a soul and lives in a body. In order to operate successfully, each of these three parts must be fed properly. The soul, or intellect, feeds on intellectual food to produce intellectual strength. The body feeds on physical food to produce physical strength. The spirit—the heart or inward part—is the real you, the part that has been reborn in Christ Jesus. It must feed on spirit food, which is

God's Word, in order to produce and develop faith. As we feast upon God's Word, our minds become renewed with His Word, and we have a fresh mental and spiritual attitude.

Likewise, you are to present your body a living sacrifice, holy, acceptable unto God. Do not allow your body to dominate your behavior, but bring it into subjection to your spirit. God's Word is healing and health to all your flesh.

Therefore, God's Word affects each part of us—spirit, soul, and body. We become vitally united to the Father, to Jesus, and to the Holy Spirit—one with Them—as we pray God's Word in every situation.

Purpose to hear, accept, and welcome the Word, and it will take root within your spirit and save your soul. Believe the Word, speak the Word, and act on the Word—it is a creative force. The Word is a double-edged sword. Often it places a demand on you to change attitudes and behaviors toward the person for whom you are praying.

Faith and Corresponding Action

Be a doer of the Word and not a hearer only, deceiving yourself. Faith without works or corresponding action is dead. Don't be a mental assenter—one who agrees that the Bible is true but never acts on it. Real faith is acting on God's Word now. You cannot build faith without practicing the Word. You cannot develop an effective prayer life that is anything but empty words unless God's Word actually has a part in your life. You are to hold fast to your confession of the Word's truthfulness. The Lord Jesus is the High Priest of your confession, and He is the guarantee of a better agreement—a more excellent and advantageous covenant.

Prayer does not cause faith to work, but faith causes prayer to work. Faith in God cannot be released while one holds grudges, is jealous, or covets things others have. James, who is traditionally the brother of Jesus, wrote, "You burn with envy and anger and are not able to obtain [the gratification, the contentment, and the happiness that you seek], so you fight and war. You do not have, because you do not ask. [Or] you do ask [God for them] and yet fail to receive, because you ask with wrong purpose and evil, selfish motives. Your intention is [when you get what you desire] to spend it in sensual pleasures."

We can spend fruitless hours in prayer if our hearts are not prepared beforehand. Preparation of the heart, the spirit, comes from meditation in the Father's Word, letting go of negative thoughts and feelings, meditating on who we are in Christ, what He is to us, and what the Holy Spirit can mean to us as we become God-inside minded.

Joshua was an effective leader, and God told him to meditate on the Word day and night, and "do according to all that is written in it. For then you shall make your way prosperous, and then you shall deal wisely and have good success." If we obey as Joshua did, we shall deal wisely and have good success.

Attend to God's Word, submit to His sayings, keep them in the center of your heart, and put away contrary talk. The Holy Spirit is a Divine Helper, and He will direct your prayer and help you pray when you don't know how. When you use God's Word in prayer, this is not something you just rush through uttering once. Do not be mistaken. There is nothing "magical" or "manipulative" about prayer—no set pattern or device that will satisfy selfish desires. Instead, you hold God's Word before Him.

Expect God's divine intervention as you choose to look at the things that are unseen, for the things that are seen are subject to change, but the unseen things are eternal.

Prayer based upon the Word rises above the senses and emotions, contacts the Author of the Word and sets His spiritual laws into motion. It is not just saying prayers that get results, but it is spending time with the Father, learning and absorbing His wisdom, drawing on His strength, being filled with His quietness, and basking in His love that bring results to our prayers.

The prayers in this book are designed to teach and train you in the art of prayer. As you pray them, you will be reinforcing the prayer armor we have been instructed to put on in Ephesians 6:11. The fabric from which the armor is made is the Word of God. We are to live by every word that proceeds from the mouth of God.

Desire the whole counsel of God because you know it changes you. By receiving that counsel, you will be "transformed (changed) by the [entire] renewal of your mind—by its new ideals and attitude—so that you may prove [for yourselves] what is the good and acceptable and perfect will of God, even the thing which is good and acceptable and perfect [in His sight for you]."

Frequently Asked Questions

"How do I pray these prayers for others?" The prayers for personal concerns may be used as intercessory prayers for others by simply praying them in the third person, changing the pronouns "I or we" to the name(s) of the person(s) for whom you are interceding and adjusting the verbs accordingly. The Holy Spirit is your helper. Remember that you cannot control another's will, but your prayers prepare the way for the individual to hear truth and understand truth.

"How many times should I pray the same prayer?" The answer is simple: You pray until you know that the answer is fixed in your heart. After that, you need to repeat the prayer whenever adverse circumstances or long delays cause you to be tempted to doubt that your prayer has been heard and your request granted.

The Word of God is your weapon against the temptation to lose heart and grow weary in your prayer life. When that Word of promise becomes fixed in your heart, you will find yourself praising and giving glory to God for the answer, even when the only evidence you have of that answer is your own faith. Reaffirming your faith enforces the triumph and victory of our Lord Jesus Christ.

"When we repeat prayers more than once, aren't we praying 'vain repetitions'?"

Obviously, such people are referring to the admonition of Jesus in Matthew 6:7, when He told His disciples: "And when you pray do not (multiply words, repeating the same ones over and over, and) heap up phrases as the Gentiles do, for they think they will be heard for their much speaking." Praying the Word of God is not praying the kind of prayer that the "heathen" pray. You will note in 1 Kings 18:25-29 the manner of prayer that was offered to the gods who could not hear. That is not the way you and I pray.

The words that we speak are not vain, but they are spirit and life. They are mighty through God to the pulling down of strongholds. We have a God whose eyes are over the righteous and whose ears are open to us: When we pray, He hears us.

You are the righteousness of God in Christ Jesus, and your prayers will avail much. They will bring salvation to the sinner, deliverance to the oppressed, healing to the sick, and prosperity to the poor. They will usher in the next move of God on the earth. In addition to affecting outward circumstances and other people, your prayers will also affect you. In the very process of praying, your life will be changed as you go from faith to faith and from glory to glory.

Your First Priority

As a Christian, your first priority is to love the Lord your God with your entire being and your neighbor as yourself.

You are called to be an intercessor, a man or woman of prayer. You are to seek the face of the Lord as you inquire, listen, meditate, and consider in the temple of the Lord.

The will of the Lord for your life is the same as it is for the life of every one of "God's set-apart ones": "Seek ye first the kingdom of God, and his righteousness; and all these things shall be added unto you."

Scripture References

James 5:16 AMP	1 Peter 3:12 AMP
Jeremiah 1:12	Hebrews 11:6
Isaiah 43:26	Philippians 4:19
Isaiah 55:11	Jeremiah 33:3
2 Chronicles 16:9	Ephesians 1
2 Corinthians 5:21	Hebrews 4:16
Psalm 100	2 Corinthians 10:4
Ephesians 6:12,18	1 Timothy 2:1 AMP
Colossians 1:9-13	John 15:8
Proverbs 15:8	Romans 8:26
1 John 5:3-5	John 6:63 AMP
Matthew 4:4	James 4:2,3
2 Timothy 2:15	Ephesians 2:10 AMP
Ephesians 3:20	Galatians 5:6
Philippians 2:16	1 Thessalonians 5:23
Ephesians 4:23,24	Romans 12:1
1 Corinthians 9:27	Proverbs 4:22

John 16:13-15

Colossians 2:10

James 2:17

Hebrews 7:22

Proverbs 4:20-24

Matthew 6:7 AMP

Matthew 6:33

John 17:21

James 1:22

Hebrews 3:1

Joshua 1:8

2 Corinthians 4:18

Romans 12:2 AMP

Hebrews 4:12 AMP

"Nothing so conclusively proves a man's ability to lead others as what he does from day to day to lead himself."

THOMAS J. WATSON

FOUNDER, IBM

Personal Affirmations

Speaking and praying affirmative prayers is a primary spiritual tool that exposes suppressed emotions and enables you to bring an unproductive thought system into obedience to the Scriptures. Romans 12:2 says, "Do not be conformed to this world (this age), [fashioned after and adapted to its external, superficial customs], but be transformed (changed) by the [entire] renewal of your mind [by its new ideals and its new attitude], so that you may prove [for yourselves] what is the good and acceptable and perfect will of God, even the thing which is good and acceptable and perfect [in His sight for you]."

Affirmations:

- I love the Lord, my God, with all my heart and with all my soul and with all my mind (intellect).

- I am submitted to Jesus, who is Lord over my spirit, my soul, and my body.

- Jesus has been made unto me wisdom, righteousness, sanctification, and redemption.

- I can do all things through Christ who strengthens me.

- The Lord is my Shepherd. I do not want. My God supplies all my need according to His riches in glory in Christ Jesus.

- I am care-free and do not fret or have anxiety about anything.

- I hear the voice of the Good Shepherd. I hear my Father's voice, and the voice of a stranger I will not follow. I roll my works upon the Lord. I commit and trust them wholly to Him. He will cause my thoughts to become agreeable to His will, and so shall my plans be established and succeed.

- I am the body of Christ. I am redeemed from the curse because Jesus bore my sicknesses and carried my diseases in His own body. By His stripes I am healed. I forbid any sickness or disease to operate in my body. Every organ, every tissue of my body functions in the perfection in which God created it to function. I honor God and bring glory to Him in my body.

- I have the mind of Christ and hold the thoughts, feelings, and purposes of His heart. I am a believer and not a doubter. I hold fast to my confession of faith. I choose to walk by faith and practice faith. My faith comes by hearing, and hearing by the Word of God. Jesus is the Author and the Developer of my faith.

- The love of God has been shed abroad in my heart by the Holy Spirit, and His love abides in me richly. I keep myself in the kingdom of light, in love, in the Word; and the wicked one touches me not. I tread over all the power of the enemy. He is a defeated foe. My shield of faith quenches his every fiery dart. Greater is He that is in me than he that is in the world.

- I am delivered from this present evil world. I am seated with Christ in heavenly places. I reside in the kingdom of God's dear Son. The law of the Spirit of life in Christ Jesus has made me free from the law of sin and death.

- I fear not, for God has given me a spirit of power, of love, and of a sound mind. God is on my side. I am a world-overcomer because I am born of God. I represent the Father and Jesus well. I am a useful member in the body of Christ. I am His workmanship recreated in Christ Jesus. My Father God is all the while effectually at work in me both to will and do His good pleasure.

- I let the Word dwell in me richly. He who began a good work in me will continue until the day of Christ.

Scripture References

Matthew 22:37 AMP	Philippians 2:9-11
1 Corinthians 1:30	Philippians 4:13
Psalm 23	Philippians 4:19
Philippians 4:6	1 Peter 5:6-7
John 10:27	Proverbs 16:3

Galatians 3:13

1 Peter 2:24

1 Corinthians 2:16

Hebrews 11:6

Hebrews 12:2

1 John 4:16

Psalm 91:13

1 John 4:4

Ephesians 2:6

Romans 8:2

Romans 8:31

Ephesians 2:10

Colossians 3:16

Matthew 8:17

1 Corinthians 6:20

Hebrews 4:14

Romans 10:17

Romans 5:5

1 John 5:18

Ephesians 6:16

Galatians 1:4

Colossians 1:13

2 Timothy 1:7

1 John 5:4,5

Philippians 2:13

Philippians 1:6

Section I

PERSONAL PRAYERS FOR LEADERS

He that is slow to anger is better than the mighty; and he that ruleth his spirit than he that taketh a city.

Proverbs 16:32

Introduction

This first section of prayers is written for everyone in leadership. The purpose is to bring transformation and build strength of character as these prayers expose hidden or suppressed emotions, wrong thought patterns, and negative attitudes. Your thoughts are vital to your success, and prayer is a spiritual tool that produces change in you, preparing you to change things.

The prayers will give self-awareness, which is the ability to understand and find solutions to personal challenges. You will have a clear understanding of the solution to a problem or the means to reaching a goal without trial and error behavior.

The prayers are tools for gathering information until you are filled to the full, beyond satisfaction. You will see beyond the obvious to other possibilities.

The prayers will give you points for meditation, and you will witness the development of a solution or receive an answer to a perplexing situation.

The prayers will bring illumination (the Ah-Ha!), as you receive intellectual or spiritual enlightenment, knowledge, revelation, insight, and/or wisdom.

The prayers make way for the confirmation of truth and/or authority.

But when you pray, go into your [most] private room, and, closing the door, pray to your Father, who is in secret; and your Father, who sees in secret, will reward you in the open.

Matthew 6:6 AMP

"The first step to leadership is servanthood."

JOHN MAXWELL

Helping Others

Father, You have blessed me with all good things and never left me without support, and I desire to freely give that which You have so freely given me. You have called me to be a leader among the people. I am so grateful that You are helping me identify those You have chosen to be members of my staff.

Your Word declares that I have the mind of Christ; therefore I sincerely desire to do unto others as I would have them do unto me. It is my privilege and joy to help those in my government office/company/military unit/business make right choices. I esteem and look upon and am concerned for their interests as they pursue their goals. As much as possible I will strengthen and build them up in all ways.

As a child of the Light, I will walk in wisdom from above. Help me encourage, equip, and assist staff and associates to develop their strengths and skills. Holy Spirit, open my eyes that I might see and discern when they need encouragement and exhortation. I will be faithful to speak a word in due season.

Father, I send forth Your love even to those who oppose me, and with Your divine help I will be kind and do good—doing favors so that someone derives benefit from them.

As I pray and meditate on Your Word, Father, You will imprint Your laws upon my heart and inscribe them on my mind—on my inmost thoughts. With the help of the Holy

Spirit, I will do to others as I would like and desire them to do to me in the name of Jesus. Amen.

Scripture References

Luke 6:31	1 Thessalonians 5:11 AMP
1 Corinthians 14:1 AMP	Luke 6:35,36 AMP
Philippians 2:4 AMP	Ephesians 5:1,2 AMP
Ephesians 6:10	Hebrews 10:16 AMP
Romans 15:2 AMP	Luke 6:31 AMP

Speaking Positively

Father, You used the power of words to create the
heavens and the earth, and Your Word endures forever. I
have joy in giving an apt answer and know that a word
spoken at the right moment—how good it is! I choose to
speak words that generate blessings and goodwill.

Today, I speak words of wisdom. If I do not stumble in
word, I am a mature person, able also to bridle my whole
body. I renounce, reject, and repent of every word that has
ever proceeded out of my mouth against other leaders,
former government officials, and Your kingdom.

I set the course of my life for obedience, for abundance,
for wisdom, for health, and for joy. O Lord, set a guard over
my mouth; keep watch at the door of my lips. Then the
words of my mouth and my deeds shall show forth Your
righteousness and Your salvation all of my days. I guard my
mouth and my tongue that I might keep myself, my organization, my ministry, and my nation from calamity.

Your Word dwells in me richly in all wisdom, and the
words that I speak release the ability of God in my innermost
being, transforming my DNA. I speak Your Words, which
are alive in me. You are alive and working in me. So, I can
boldly say that my words are words of faith, words of power,
words of love, and words of life. They produce good things in
my life, lead people in paths of righteousness, and they can
even change the course of our nation. I choose Your Words

for my lips; Your will for my life and the lives of those under my leadership in Jesus' name. Amen.

Scripture References

Genesis 1	Proverbs 15:23
Ephesians 5:4	Proverbs 21:23
2 Timothy 2:16	Ephesians 4:27
James 3:6	James 1:6
Proverbs 8:6,7	John 6:63
2 Corinthians 5:21	Colossians 3:16
Proverbs 4:23	Philemon 6

Safe Travel

Father, in the name of Jesus, I thank You for being my shelter. I confess Jesus as my Lord, and I choose to dwell in the secret place of the Most High at all times. I shall remain stable and fixed under the shadow of the Almighty, whose power no foe can withstand.

Today, I decree that You are my refuge and my fortress. No evil shall befall me —no accident shall overtake me—no plague or calamities shall come near me. Thank You for Your angels who have special charge over me. I bless this aircraft, the pilots and everyone who is aboard. Just as the blood applied to the doorpost protected the Hebrew children, I believe that the blood of Jesus protects us as we soar through the skies.

When I am traveling, I say, "Let me pass over to the other side." I go on my way, secure and in confident trust, for my heart and mind are firmly fixed and stayed on You, and I am kept in perfect peace. When I take to the skies, You walk on the wings of the wind. I thank You for divine protection, for keeping the pilots alert mentally, emotionally, and spiritually.

At night, I sing for joy upon my bed because You sustain me. In peace I lie down and sleep, for You alone, Lord, make me dwell in safety.

Father God, You are my confidence, firm and strong. You keep my foot from being caught in a trap or hidden danger. You give me safety and ease me—Jesus is my safety!

Thank You, Father, in Jesus' name. Amen.

Scripture References

Jeremiah 1:12	Proverbs 3:23 AMP
Psalm 91:1,2 AMP	Psalm 112:7
Psalm 91:10 AMP	Isaiah 26:3
Psalm 91:11 AMP	Psalm 149:5
Psalm 34:7	Psalm 3:5
Proverbs 3:26 AMP	Psalm 4:8 AMP
Isaiah 49:25	Proverbs 3:24
Mark 4:35	Psalm 127:2

"Now that we have stated and answered the first question; let us proceed to the consideration of the second—how shall we, in particular instances, learn the dictates of our duty, and make, with accuracy, the proper distinction between right and wrong; in other words, how shall we, in particular cases, discover the will of God? We discover it by our conscience, by our reason, and by the Holy Scriptures. The law of nature and the law of revelation are both divine: they flow, though in different channels, from the same adorable source. It is, indeed, preposterous to separate them from each other. The object of both is—to discover the will of God—and both are necessary for the accomplishment of that end."

JAMES WILSON

(FOUNDING FATHER AND ONE OF THE
ORIGINAL SUPREME COURT JUSTICES)

Knowing God's Will

O my God, I desire to do Your will. Your law is within my heart. In Jesus' name, I thank You for instructing me in the way I should go and for guiding me with Your eye. I give heed to Your instruction. My trust is in You, and I am prospering. I am blessed.

You make known to me Your will, Your plan, and Your purpose for my life that I might be a blessing to others. I hear the voice of the Good Shepherd, for I know You and follow You. You lead me in the paths of righteousness for Your name's sake.

In my heart I have planned my course, but I am relying on You, my Lord, to determine my steps. Before the foundation of the world You chose me and ordained my paths. My will is to do Your will.

Thank You, Father, that Jesus was made unto me wisdom. Confusion is not a part of my life. I do not entertain confusion or submit to popular opinion that is contrary to righteousness. I trust in You and lean not unto my own understanding. As I acknowledge You in all of my ways, You are directing my paths. I believe that as I trust in You completely, You will show me the path of life; You will show me how to influence others and restore this country to wholeness.

As I follow you, my path is growing brighter and brighter until it reaches the full light of day, and I will lead men and

women in paths of righteousness for Your name's sake and
for Your glory.

Amen.

Scripture References

Psalm 40:8

Psalm 32:8

John 10:3,4

Psalm 23:3

Proverbs 4:18

Ephesians 5:19

Proverbs 16:9

1 Corinthians 1:30

1 Corinthians 14:33

Proverbs 3:5,6

Psalm 16:11

"The very essence of leadership is [that] you have a vision. It's got to be a vision you articulate clearly and forcefully on every occasion. You can't blow an uncertain trumpet."

THEODORE HESBURGH

FORMER PRESIDENT OF NOTRE DAME UNIVERSITY

Developing Better Communication Skills

Father, with all my heart I desire that my communication will continually be motivated by love for others. Show "me" to me so that I might change wrong attitudes and let go of prejudice and bad feelings towards others. Bring everything to the light. Expose insecurities that push me into being self-defensive; expose partisan bias that would exalt itself above Your purposes.

When anything is exposed and reproved by the light, it is made visible and clear; and where everything is visible and clear, there is light. Your light dispels the darkness, and I have no need for self-aggrandizement and self-promotion. I exchange my opinions for Your direction.

Teach me to guard my heart with all diligence, for out of it flow the very issues of life. I choose to speak the truth in love wherever I may be, in all my relationships. Thank You for giving me discernment as I listen to the ideas and opinions of others, especially when they are different than mine.

I will honestly esteem others and value their opinions, avoiding stupid and foolish controversies and dissensions and wrangling. The power of life and death is in the tongue, and You said that I would eat the fruit of it. A word out of my mouth may seem of no account, but it can accomplish nearly anything—or destroy it!

Father, forgive me for criticizing and judging others harshly. Forgive me for those times when I have knowingly or unknowingly twisted the truth to make myself sound wise. Sometimes my words have contributed to things falling apart. Sometimes my human anger was misdirected and worked unrighteousness. I thank You for forgiving me, and I forgive myself. You are cleansing me from all unrighteousness.

Father, I ask for wisdom that is from above and submit to the wisdom that begins with a holy life and is characterized by getting along with others. Use me as Your instrument in developing a God-fearing, healthy community. I will enjoy its results only if I do the hard work of getting along with others, treating them with dignity and honor.

My tongue is as choice silver, and my lips feed and guide many. I open my mouth in skillful and godly wisdom to give counsel and clear instructions.

Lord, You are my God and I love You with all my heart, soul, and mind. And I will love others as well as I love myself. In the name of Jesus I pray, amen.

Scripture References

1 John 3:1	Titus 3:9
Ephesians 4:29 NIV	Matthew 6:6
Psalm 45:1 AMP	Hebrews 11:6 AMP
Proverbs 3:3 AMP	Ephesians 5:13 AMP
Proverbs 8:6-8 AMP	Proverbs 4:23
Proverbs 10:20,21 AMP	Ephesians 4:15
Proverbs 31:26 AMP	Proverbs 18:21

Romans 8:31-39 NIV

Hebrews 2:11 NIV

John 15:15 NIV

John 14:26

Revelation 12:11

James 3:5,6 THE MESSAGE

James 3:9-16 THE MESSAGE

James 3:17

James 3:17,18 THE MESSAGE

Preparing for Travel

Today, I confess God's Word over our travel plans.

As my family/associates and I prepare to travel, I rejoice in the promises that Your Word holds for protection and safety of the righteous. Father, I trust in You and dwell in Your protection. Believing in the written Word of God, I speak peace, safety, and success over the travel plans for my associates/my family, in Jesus' name.

As a child of God, our path of travel is preserved, and angels keep charge over us. We will proceed with our travel plans without fear of accidents, problems, or any type of frustrations. Lord, thank You for delivering us from every type of evil and preserving us for Your kingdom. I stand confident that our travel plans will not be disrupted or confused.

Thank You, Father, that in every situation You are there to protect us. No matter by what means of transportation we choose to travel, You have redeemed us and will protect us. The earth and all things on it are under Your command. You are my Heavenly Father. Through my faith in You, I have the power to tread over the power of the enemy. No food or water will harm us when we arrive at our destination.

Father, I give You the glory in this situation. Thank You that as I keep Your ways before me, we will be safe. Your mercy is upon me and my associates/family, and our travels will be safe. Thank You, Father, for Your guidance and safety—You are worthy of all praise! Amen.

Scripture References

Isaiah 55:11

Jeremiah 1:12

Psalm 4:8

Psalm 91:1

Proverbs 18:10

Proverbs 29:25

Mark 11:23,24

Proverbs 2:8

Psalm 91:11,12

Timothy 4:18

Philippians 4:7

2 Timothy 1:7

Isaiah 43:1-3

2 Timothy 4:18

Hosea 2:18

Luke 10:19

Psalm 91:13

Luke 21:18

Mark 16:18

Matthew 18:18

John 14:13 2

Daniel 9:18

Luke 1:50

"Let no one come to you without leaving better and happier."

MOTHER TERESA

Giving and Finding Favor

Father, You make Your face to shine upon me and enlighten me, and You are gracious (kind, merciful and giving favor) to me. Thank You for bestowing Your favor upon me. I seek Your kingdom and Your righteousness and diligently seek good. I am a blessing to You, Lord, and a blessing to _____ (name them: family, neighbors, business associates, constituents, etc.). Grace (favor) is with me, and I love You, Father, because You first loved me.

Because You extend favor, honor, and love to me, I release Your love and favor to others. Freely I have received and freely I give. You are pouring out upon me the spirit of favor. You crown me with glory and honor, for I am Your child—Your workmanship created in Christ Jesus unto good works.

I am growing in grace and the knowledge of Jesus Christ, who is my Lord. I continue to wax strong in spirit. Father, I thank You for giving me knowledge and skill in all learning and wisdom. You bring me to find favor, compassion, and loving-kindness with _____ (names).

Father, I am filled with Your fullness—rooted and grounded in love. You are doing exceeding abundantly, above all that I ask or think, for Your mighty power is taking over in my life.

Thank You, Father, that I give favor to others, and I am increasing in favor with You and with other people.

In Jesus' name I pray, amen.

Scripture References

Numbers 6:25 AMP

Deuteronomy 28:13

Matthew 6:33

Proverbs 11:27

Ephesians 6:24

Zechariah 12:10 AMP

Psalm 8:5 AMP

Ephesians 2:10 AMP

Luke 2:40

Daniel 1:17

Daniel 1:9 AMP

Esther 2:15 AMP

Ephesians 3:17,19,20

Luke 2:52

"I have been driven many times upon my knees by the overwhelming conviction that I had nowhere else to go. My own wisdom and that of all about me seemed insufficient for that day."

ABRAHAM LINCOLN

Trusting God's Leadership

Father, I thank You for instructing me and teaching me in the way I should go, and I am confident that You are guiding me with Your eye. I thank You for divine guidance and leadership concerning Your will, Your plan, and Your purpose for my life. I do hear the voice of the Good Shepherd, for I know You and follow You. You lead me in the paths of righteousness for Your name's sake.

In the name of Jesus, I refuse to be conformed to this world (this age), [fashioned after and adapted to its external, superficial customs]. Instead I submit to transformation by the [entire] renewal of my mind [by its new ideals and its new attitude], so that I may prove [for myself] what is Your good and acceptable and perfect will, even the thing which is good and acceptable and perfect [in Your sight for me].

Thank You, Father, that my path is growing brighter and brighter until it reaches the full light of day. As I follow You, Lord, I believe my path is becoming clearer each day. Thank You, Father, that Jesus was made unto me wisdom. Confusion is far from me. I trust in You and lean not to my own understanding. As I acknowledge You in all my ways, You direct my paths. I believe that as I trust in You completely, You will show me the path of life.

Thank You, Father, in Jesus' name. Amen.

Scripture References

Psalm 32:8

John 10:3,4

Psalm 23:3

Romans 12:2 AMP

Proverbs 4:18

1 Corinthians 1:30

Proverbs 3:5,6

Psalm 16:11

"Far and away the best prize that life offers is the chance to work hard at work worth doing."

THEODORE ROOSEVELT

Praying for Excellence

Lord, help me today to be astute in all that I do. I will do my very best. Help me to be the most valuable, godly representative possible, one who is sensitive to the needs of others. I purpose to perform my duties with a spirit of excellence, to do all that is required of me, and even above and beyond that which is required of me, that I may be a blessing to others and an effective leader.

Lord, I purpose in my heart to fulfill my duties to the best of my ability. I will complete my responsibilities and be a consistent and effective worker. If I make a mistake, I will be open and honest and forthright, admitting it and doing all that I can to correct it.

I make a commitment to do my job humbly and quietly, effectively and efficiently. I will speak truly, deal truly, and live truly. I purpose to be conscientious and trustworthy in all my business dealings.

I will do my best to establish and maintain good relationships with all my contacts and co-workers. I am committed to be a faithful, devoted representative. Whatever my hand touches I will do with all my might, with all my energy, and with all that is within me. I will do everything in my power to become a productive leader. In Jesus' name I pray, amen.

Scripture References

Proverbs 16:3 NIV

Daniel 5:12 AMP

Proverbs 17:27 AMP

Proverbs 10:4

Proverbs 22:29 NIV

Romans 12:17 NIV

Colossians 3:17

Proverbs 28:20

2 Chronicles 16:9

1 John 4:4

Psalm 75:6,7

"The ultimate measure of a man is not where he stands in moments of comfort, but where he stands at times of challenge and controversy."

MARTIN LUTHER KING JR.

Praying at the Close of the Day

Prayer for the Married Person

Father, I thank You that I am laying aside the cares and emotional baggage of the day's activities. Whatever responsibilities, problems, or situations I faced, however difficult the day may have been for me, I release it all to You. I submit my mind and emotions to the control of the Holy Spirit.

With the same zeal, enthusiasm, and fervor that I started this day, I now turn toward home. I am filled with gratitude and thanksgiving for my family. Father, grant me a refreshing now, for the second part of my day. Your joy overflows in my heart, and as I enter the doorway of my home, I bring with me joy and peace and life.

Lord, You are the strength of my life: spirit, soul, and body. The light in my eyes will rejoice the hearts of my family. I have a smile on my face and joy in my heart because You have made me glad. I look forward to a wonderful evening with my loved ones. I love You because You first loved me, and I love my family even as I love myself.

Lord, help me never—under any circumstances, either by word or deed—to be condescending or to insinuate that I think less of the responsibilities of my marriage partner than I do my own. I choose to encourage and strengthen my spouse and to be their best friend and closest confidant.

Thank You for physical strength so I can enjoy my children. I am sensitive to their conversations and attuned to the events of their day, and I thank You for helping me see things from their perspectives and viewpoints.

Lord, I celebrate the victories my spouse and children have experienced today and choose to respond with excitement and enthusiasm to whatever made them happy. I am tenderhearted and sympathetic to whatever challenges they had to face in their world, and with Your help, Lord, I purpose to instill within them a confidence, a trust, and surety in You. I will teach them to lean not to their own understanding but in all their ways to acknowledge You.

Thank You for the gift of Your Holy Spirit to empower me for the work You have called me to do and to fulfill the role at home that You have entrusted to me.

In Jesus' name I pray, amen.

Scripture References

Psalm 19:14	Joel 3:10
Psalm 28:7	Ephesians 4:32
Proverbs 17:22	1 Timothy 4:14
Isaiah 40:29 NIV	Proverbs 15:23 AMP
Isaiah 41:10 AMP	Romans 13:10 AMP
Psalm 127:3-5	Acts 1:8

Prayer for the Single Person

Father, I thank You for this day and all that I have been able to accomplish. Thank You for Your guiding presence, Your wisdom, and Your counsel.

Lord, I thank You that I have learned not to take any of the stresses or unresolved problems of the day home with me, but to leave them at the office. Whatever responsibilities, problems, or situations I had to face there, however difficult some parts of the day may have been for me, I give it all to You. By an act of my will, I choose not to think about it, meditate on it, or allow it to control my life.

With the same zeal, enthusiasm, and fervor that I started this day, I now turn toward home. Father, grant me a refreshing now, for the second part of my day. Thank You that Your joy overflows in my heart. As I enter my home, let me bring with me joy, peace, and life—not misery, frustration, and fatigue.

Lord, I ask You to strengthen me: spirit, soul, and body. Fill my heart with Your love and grace. Clear my mind of the cobwebs of the day. Help me to enjoy whatever plans or activities I have arranged for this afternoon or evening. Thank You for friends, neighbors, and family that are a part of my life and the opportunities we have to enjoy one another.

You have taught me the importance of rest and balance in my life, so I will not over-commit, over-schedule, or over-work simply because I have the time. I ask that You continue to help me listen for Your voice as I learn what things should have my time and attention.

Help me never to speak ill about anyone in my workplace or say anything that will give them wrong thoughts or ideas or attitudes toward my work. Thank You for the gift of Your Holy Spirit to empower me for the work You have called me to do. Thank You for the full, rich, and rewarding life that I have because of You.

In Jesus' name I pray, amen.

Scripture References

Psalm 19:14

Psalm 28:7

Proverbs 17:22

Isaiah 40:29 NIV

Isaiah 41:10 AMP

Psalm 127:3-5

Joel 3:10

Ephesians 4:32

1 Timothy 4:14

Proverbs 15:23 AMP

Romans 13:10 AMP

Acts 1:8

"It is impossible to account for the
creation of the universe without the
agency of a Supreme Being."

GEORGE WASHINGTON

Encouragement From God

Father, I love You with all my heart and with all my soul and with all my mind (intellect), and I shall love my neighbor as [I do] myself.

You created my inmost being and I am one with You. You knit me together in my mother's womb. I praise You because I am fearfully and wonderfully made. Your works are wonderful; I know that full well. I accept myself because You have received, welcomed, and accepted me in the Beloved.

Before You formed me in the womb You knew and approved of me [as Your chosen instrument], and before I was born You set me apart, consecrated me; [and] You appointed me for a special work. You know me by name, and I have found favor in Your sight because of Your great love.

With the help of the Holy Spirit, I rate my ability with sober judgment, according to the degree of faith apportioned to me. You have given me Your creative ability, and in Christ I am capable, competent, and qualified to be all that You created me to be. Even in my weaknesses Your grace is sufficient.

The power of Christ rests upon me. I resist feelings and thoughts of rejection because I am accepted, loved, and favored by You, the Most High God.

Thank You for prompting me to help others feel good about themselves by encouraging, supporting, and praising them as we work together to achieve the goals of this organization. I give you all the glory for any accomplishments that have been credited to me.

In Jesus' name I pray, amen.

Scripture References

Matthew 22:37-39 AMP   Romans 12:3-6 AMP

Isaiah 43:1 AMP   1 John 4:18

Jeremiah 1:5 AMP   Psalm 139:13,14 NIV

Exodus 33:12 AMP   Ephesians 1:6

2 Corinthians 12:9,10

"In the swift rush of great events, we find ourselves groping to know the full sense and meaning of these times in which we live. In our quest of understanding, we beseech God's guidance."

DWIGHT EISENHOWER

Growing in Wisdom

Father, I desire to receive wisdom and discipline. I ask for the ability to understand words of insight. By Your grace, I am acquiring a disciplined and prudent life, doing what is right and just and fair.

Thank You for giving me prudence, knowledge, and discretion. As a wise person I listen and add to my learning, and as a discerning person I accept guidance [so that I may be able to steer my course rightly].

Thank You that I understand proverbs and parables, the sayings and riddles of the wise. My delight is in the law of the Lord and I meditate on it day and night. In a multitude of counselors there is safety. I surround myself with wise counselors and submit myself to the constant ministry of transformation by the Holy Spirit.

In Jesus' name I pray, amen.

Scripture References

Proverbs 1:2-7 NIV   Proverbs 1:5 AMP

Psalm 1   2 Corinthians 3:18

"Whether you think you can or whether you think you can't, you're right!"

HENRY FORD

Being Well-Balanced

Father, in the name of Jesus, I come boldly to Your throne of grace to receive mercy and find grace to help in time of need.

Forgive me for getting caught up in my own pride. Sometimes I behave as though I am indispensable at home, at the office, at church, and in other situations. I become irritable and fatigued, feeling that no one appreciates all that I do. Today, I am stepping back and taking a personal inventory. Holy Spirit, help my spirit, which is the candle of the Lord, search out all the inward parts of my being.

There is a time for everything and a season for every activity under heaven. With Your power at work in me I will keep my priorities in order, that I may fulfill my call and responsibilities at home and at work. I take time to find rest—relief, ease, refreshment, recreation, and blessed quiet—for my soul. Putting first things first, I order my day aright and give my attention to Your Word through reading, prayer, and meditation.

I cast the whole of my care [all my anxieties, all my worries, all my concerns, once and for all] on You, for You care for me affectionately and care about me watchfully. I affirm that I am well-balanced (temperate, sober of mind), vigilant, and cautious at all times; for that enemy of mine, the devil, roams around like a lion roaring [in fierce hunger], seeking someone to seize upon and devour.

In the name of Jesus I resist the enemy, standing firm in the faith because I know that my brothers throughout the world are undergoing the same kind of sufferings. And the God of all grace, who called me to His eternal glory in Christ, after I have suffered a little while, will Himself restore me and make me strong, firm, and steadfast.

To You be the dominion (power, authority, rule) forever and ever. Amen (so be it).

Scripture References

Hebrews 4:16

Proverbs 20:27

2 Corinthians 6:14

Matthew 11:28-30 PHILLIPS

Ecclesiastes 3:1 NIV

Matthew 11:29 AMP

1 Peter 5:7-11 AMP

Living Free From Worry

Father, I thank You that I have been delivered from the power of darkness and translated into the kingdom of Your dear Son. I commit to live free from worry, in the name of Jesus, for the law of the Spirit of life in Christ Jesus has made me free from the law of sin and death.

I humble myself under Your mighty hand, that in due time You may exalt me. I cast the whole of my cares of _____ [name them]—all my anxieties, all my worries, all my concerns, once and for all—on You. You care for me affectionately and care about me watchfully. You sustain me. You will never allow the consistently righteous to be moved—made to slip, fall, or fail!

Father, I delight myself in You, and You perfect that which concerns me. I cast down imaginations (reasonings) and every high thing that exalts itself against the knowledge of You and bring into captivity every thought to the obedience of Christ. I lay aside every weight and the sin of worry, which does try so easily to beset me. I run with patience the race that is set before me, looking unto Jesus, the author and finisher of my faith.

I choose to trust You in every situation, and I know that You will not fail one word of Your promise. I live by the faith of the Son of God and affirm daily that I am secure in You.

I thank You, Father, that You are able to keep that which I have committed unto You. I think on (fix my mind on) those things that are true, honest, just, pure, lovely, of good report, virtuous, and deserving of praise. My heart is free from worry because I abide in Your words, and Your words abide in me.

Father, I remember who I am in Christ Jesus. I look into the perfect law of liberty and continue therein, being a doer of the Word and thus I am blessed in my doing!

Thank You, Father, that in You I am carefree. I walk in the peace which passes all understanding, in Jesus' name!

Scripture References

Colossians 1:13	Hebrews 12:1,2
Romans 8:2	2 Timothy 1:12
1 Peter 5:6,7	Philippians 4:8
Psalm 55:22	John 14:1
Psalm 138:8	James 1:22-25
2 Corinthians 10:5	Philippians 4:6
Galatians 2:20	

"King David of Israel gives the most extraordinary health report that history records. David says, 'There was not one feeble one among their tribes.' Such historic data should go far to convince the world of our day that an absolute trust in God is not only a safe policy but a most scientific guarantee of national health."

JOHN G. LAKE

Living in Health

Father, in the name of Jesus, because of Your great and precious promises, I ask You to heal me. It is written that the prayer of faith will save the sick, and the Lord will raise them up. And if I have committed sins, I will be forgiven. I let go of all unforgiveness, resentment, anger, and bad feelings toward anyone.

My body is the temple of the Holy Spirit, and I desire to be in good health. I seek truth that will make me free—both spiritual and natural (good eating habits, medications if necessary, and appropriate rest and exercise). You bought me at a price, and I desire to glorify You in my spirit and my body—they both belong to You.

Thank You, Father, for sending Your Word to heal me and deliver me from all my destructions. Jesus, You are the Word who became flesh and dwelt among us. You bore my griefs (pains) and carried my sorrows (sickness). You were pierced through for my transgressions and crushed for my iniquities; the chastening for my well-being fell upon You, and by Your scourging I am healed.

Father, I give attention to Your words and incline my ear to Your sayings. I will not let them depart from my sight, but I will keep them in the midst of my heart, for they are life and health to my whole body.

Since the Spirit of Him who raised Jesus from the dead dwells in me, He who raised Christ from the dead will also give life to my mortal body through His Spirit who dwells in me.

Bless the Lord, oh my soul, and forget not all His benefits; who forgives all our iniquities and heals all our diseases. You have healed me from the oppression of the devil. I am vibrant, robust, cheerful, and healthy!

Thank You that I will prosper and be in health, even as my soul prospers. Amen.

Scripture References

James 5:15 NKJV

1 Corinthians 6:19,20

Psalm 107:20

John 1:14

Isaiah 53:4,5 NASB

Proverbs 4:21,22 NASB

Psalm 103:3-5 NASB

Romans 8:11 NKJV

3 John 2

"Example is not the main thing in influencing others, it is the only thing."

ALBERT SCHWEITZER

Developing Patience

Father, in the name of Jesus, I thank You for the Holy Spirit, who helps me develop and exercise patience, a fruit of the Spirit. I will remember that the end of a matter is better than its beginning, and patience is better than pride. I resist the temptation to be quickly provoked in my spirit, for anger resides in the lap of fools.

I desire to live wisely with a sense of responsibility, as one who knows the meaning and purpose of life. I purpose to make the best use of my time, despite all the difficulties of these days.

I choose to count it all joy when I fall into various trials, knowing that the testing of my faith produces patience. I realize that these come to test my faith and to produce in me the quality of endurance. I purpose to let the process go on until that endurance is fully developed, and I will find that I have become a person of mature character with the right sort of independence.

Father, Your grace (Your favor and loving-kindness and mercy) is enough for me [sufficient against any danger and enables me to bear trouble maturely]; for Your strength and power are made perfect (fulfilled and completed) and show themselves most effective in [my] weakness.

And if, in the process, I do not know how to meet any particular problem, I ask You, Father, for wisdom. You give generously to all who ask without making them feel guilty—and I am quite sure that the necessary wisdom will be given me.

I am still, knowing that You are God. I am calm and serene as I wait upon You. I choose to be patient and pleasant, and I accept that which I cannot change. You are my Light and my Salvation, my Patience.

As I live this new life, I pray that I will be strengthened from Your glorious power, so that I will find myself able to pass through any experience and endure it with joy. In Jesus' name I pray, amen.

Scripture References

Ecclesiastes 7:8,9 NIV

Ephesians 5:15 PHILLIPS

James 1:2,3 NKJV

2 Corinthians 12:9 AMP

James 1:3-5 PHILLIPS

Colossians 1:11 PHILLIPS

"My hope in the One who created us all sustains me: He is an ever present help in trouble…. When I was extremely depressed, He raised me with His right hand, saying, 'O man of little faith, get up, it is I; do not be afraid.'"

CHRISTOPHER COLUMBUS

Overcoming Intimidation

Father, I come to You in the name of Jesus, confessing that intimidation has caused me to stumble. I ask Your forgiveness for thinking of myself as inferior, for I am created in Your image, and I am Your workmanship. Jesus said that Your kingdom is within me. Therefore, the power that raised Jesus from the dead dwells in me and causes me to face life with hope and divine energy.

You, Lord, are my light and my salvation; whom shall I fear? You are the strength of my life; of whom shall I be afraid?

Father, You have said that You will never leave me or forsake me. Therefore, I can say without any doubt or fear that You are my Helper, and I am not afraid of anything that a mere human being can do to me. I am free from the fear of other people and the pressure of public opinion.

Father, You have given me a spirit of power and of love and of a calm and well-balanced mind of discipline and self-control.

Greater is He who is in me than he who is in the world. In all situations I remain calm, masterful, and at peace with God and who I am in Christ. If God be for me, who can be against me?

In Jesus' name I pray, amen.

Scripture References

1 John 1:9

Hebrews 13:5,6

Genesis 1:27

1 John 4:4

Ephesians 2:10

Romans 8:31

Luke 17:21

2 Timothy 1:7 AMP

Ephesians 1:19,20

Philippians 4:13 NIV

Colossians 1:29

Proverbs 29:25

Psalm 27:1

"On my advanced stage of life, a life worn out almost in the constant cares of office, I think it my duty to retire from the busy concerns of public affairs; that at the evening of my days, I may sweeten their decline by devoting myself with less avocation and more attention to the duties of religion, the service of my God, and preparation for a future and happier state of existence, in which pleasing employment I shall not cease to remember by county, and to make it my ardent prayer that Heaven will not fail to bless her with the choicest favors."

JONATHAN TRUMBULL

(GOVERNOR OF THE STATE OF CONNECTICUT,
FROM HIS LETTER OF RESIGNATION
AT THE AGE OF 73)

Wise Conversation

Father, I desire to give and receive feedback, and purpose to live truly, deal truly, and speak truly. I decree that my conversation and my behavior will issue from the fountain of wisdom that comes down from heaven. Through wisdom I will motivate others to improve their performance and take pleasure in their work.

Jesus has been made unto me wisdom that is first of all pure and full of quiet gentleness, peace-loving and courteous, and allows discussion. Give me the grace to listen when others speak, and help me understand their viewpoints and opinions. I pray that my words will be full of grace, even when I disagree. I will be wholehearted and straightforward in all my negotiations. Motivated by wisdom I yield to reason.

My mind is fixed on whatever is true and honorable and just and pure and lovely and admirable. I model my conduct on what I have learned from the Scriptures, and the God of peace is with me.

It is my prayer that I will overflow more and more with love for others, while at the same time growing in spiritual knowledge and insight, for I want always to see clearly the difference between right and wrong and to be inwardly clean. May I always be doing those good, kind things that show I am a child of God, for this will bring much praise and glory to You.

Father, I submit to Your Word, which is living and active. Sharper than any two-edged sword; it penetrates even to dividing soul and spirit, joints and marrow; it judges the thoughts and attitudes of my heart.

Surely You desire truth in the inner parts; You teach me wisdom in the inmost place. Cleanse me with hyssop, and I will be clean; wash me, and I will be whiter than snow. In Jesus' name I pray, amen.

Scripture References

Ephesians 4:15 AMP

Philippians 4:8,9 PHILLIPS

Hebrews 4:12 NIV

1 Peter 1:22 NKJV

James 3

Psalm 51:6,7 NIV

Philippians 1:9-11 TLB

Leading with Gentleness

Father, I desire to be a leader controlled by Your wisdom, which is full of quiet gentleness. Reveal to me by Your Spirit how to be equitable, fair, moderate, and forbearing in all my dealings. I desire to look at situations humanely and reasonably rather than insisting on the letter of the law.

In the name of Jesus, I will not be combative but gentle and kind and considerate, not quarrelsome but forbearing and peaceable, and not a lover of money. I seek to be submissive, obedient, prepared, and willing to do any upright and honorable work.

I will not slander or abuse or speak evil of anyone (my associates, customers, friends, family members, or competitors). I avoid contentiousness. In the name of Jesus, I am forbearing (yielding, gentle, and conciliatory), and I affirm that I will show unqualified courtesy toward everybody.

Father, I desire that my administration of this organization not be burdensome or irksome to others. I purpose to be gentle among my employees and staff.

I recognize that gentleness is love in action—being considerate, meeting the needs of others, allowing time for the other person to talk, and being willing to learn. Help me maintain a gentle attitude in my relationships with others.

In Jesus' name I pray, amen.

Scripture References

James 3:17 TLB

Titus 3:1-3 AMP

1 Timothy 3:3

1 Thessalonians 2:7 NIV

"The measure of a life, after all, is not its duration but its donation."

CORRIE TEN BOOM

Home and Family

Father, I thank You that You have blessed me and my family with all spiritual blessings in Christ Jesus.

Through skillful and godly wisdom is my house (my life, my home, my family) built, and by understanding it is established [on a sound and good foundation]. And by knowledge shall its chambers [of every area] be filled with all precious and pleasant riches—great [priceless] treasure. The house of the [uncompromisingly] righteous shall stand. Prosperity and welfare are in my house, in the name of Jesus.

My house is securely built. It is founded on a rock—revelation knowledge of Your Word, Father. Jesus is its Cornerstone. Jesus is Lord of my household. Jesus is our Lord—spirit, soul, and body.

Whatever may be our task, we work at it heartily (from the soul), as [something done] for You, Lord, and not for men. We love each other with the God-kind of love, and we dwell in peace. Our home is committed to You [deposited into Your charge, entrusted to Your protection and care].

Father, I know not what others may do, but as for me and my house, we will serve the Lord! Hallelujah!

In Jesus' name I pray, amen.

Scripture References

Ephesians 1:3

Proverbs 24:3,4 AMP

Proverbs 15:6 AMP

Acts 16:31 AMP

Philippians 2:10,11 AMP

Colossians 3:23 AMP

"Education is useless without
the Bible."

NOAH WEBSTER

"A great man stands on God."

RALPH WALDO EMERSON

Children at School

Father, I confess Your Word this day concerning my children as they pursue their education and training at school. You are effectually at work in them [energizing and creating in them the power and desire] both to will and to work for Your good pleasure. They are the head and not the tail, above only and not beneath.

I pray that my children will find favor, good understanding, and high esteem in Your sight and in the judgment of their teachers and classmates. I ask You to give my children wisdom and understanding as knowledge is presented to them in all fields of study and endeavor.

Father, thank You for giving them the aptitude for every kind of learning, that they may be well informed, quick to understand, and qualified to serve You. I ask You to help us (the parents and our children) remember that the fear of the Lord is the beginning of knowledge.

Thank You that my children have the appetite of the diligent; they are abundantly supplied with educational resources, and their thoughts are those of the steadily diligent, which tend only to achievement. Thank You that they are growing in wisdom and knowledge.

I will not cease to pray for my children, asking that they be filled with the knowledge of Your will, bearing fruit in every good work.

Father, I thank You that my children have divine protection since they dwell in the secret place of the Most High. They trust and find their refuge in You and stand rooted and grounded in Your love. They shall not be led astray by philosophies of men and teaching that is contrary to truth. You are their shield and buckler, protecting them from all attacks or threats. Thank You for the angels whom You have assigned to them, that accompany and defend and preserve them in all their ways [of obedience and service].

My children are established in Your love, which turns all fear out of doors and expels every trace of terror.

I pray that my children's teachers will be men and women of integrity. Give them understanding hearts and wisdom in order that they may walk in the ways of piety and virtue, revering Your holy name.

In Jesus' name I pray, amen.

Scripture References

Philippians 2:13 AMP

Deuteronomy 28:1,2,13 AMP

Proverbs 3:4 AMP

1 Kings 4:29

Daniel 1:4 NIV

Proverbs 1:7 NIV

Colossians 1:9,10 NIV, TLB, AMP

Psalm 91:1,2 AMP

Ephesians 3:17

Ephesians 4:14

Psalm 91:3-11 AMP

1 John 4:18 AMP

Proverbs 21:5 RSV

Making Decisions

Devotional Reading

And let the peace (soul harmony which comes) from
Christ rule (act as umpire continually) in your hearts
[deciding and settling with finality all questions that arise
in your minds, in that peaceful state] to which as
[members of Christ's] one body you were also called [to
live]. And be thankful (appreciative), [giving praise to
God always].

Colossians 3:15 AMP

Meditation

Whether your business decisions are made by you alone
or by a board of trustees, pray the following for assurance and
confidence. Pray the same prayer also for those to whom you
have delegated the authority to make decisions, entrusting
them to God, who directs their steps. Sometimes mistakes
will be made, but the Lord is bigger than our mistakes.

Prayer

Father, I realize that before I can love others as You have
instructed me, I must love myself. Help me to speak truly,
deal truly, and live truly in harmony with You, myself, and
the members of my organization. I am Your workmanship,
re-created in Christ Jesus, that I may do those good works
which You, Lord, predestined (planned beforehand) for me

[taking paths which You prepared ahead of time], that I should walk in them [living the good life which You prearranged and made ready for me to live].

Help me to give attention to a matter before I act, take time to plan and strategize, and listen to wise counsel. I weigh and consider advice before taking action. I accept my responsibility as a leader (owner, employer, supervisor, manager, chairman of the board) to make the final decision concerning company issues, business transactions, and corporate policies. I trust in You with all my heart and lean not on my own understanding; in all my ways I acknowledge You, and You direct my paths. I look to You to cause my thoughts to be agreeable to Your will, that I might make wise and healthy choices.

Give me the courage to make decisions that are in agreement with Your purpose and plan for my life and the lives of my associates. My yes shall be yes—my no, no.

Strengthened with Your power and might, I am concerned with the interests of others and desire to do unto others as I would have them do unto me. I am walking uprightly before You; therefore, I consider, direct, and establish my way [with the confidence of integrity].

You are my confidence, and You keep my foot from being snared. Your love is shed abroad in my heart. I love my neighbors—my fellow workers—as myself, and make decisions with their welfare in mind.

In Jesus' name I pray, amen.

Scripture References

Romans 13:9 AMP

Ephesians 4:15 AMP

Ephesians 2:10 AMP

Psalm 139:14

Proverbs 11:14

Proverbs 3:5,6

Proverbs 16:3 AMP

Romans 8:28 NIV

Matthew 5:37 AMP

Colossians 1:11

Philippians 2:3,4 AMP

Matthew 7:12 AMP

Proverbs 21:29 AMP

Proverbs 3:26 NIV

Romans 5:5

Luke 10:27

Seeking Wisdom

Devotional Reading

My son, if you accept my words
and store up my commands within you,

turning your ear to wisdom
and applying your heart to understanding,

and if you call out for insight
and cry aloud for understanding,

and if you look for it as silver
and search for it as for hidden treasure,

then you will understand the fear of the Lord
and find the knowledge of God.

For the Lord gives wisdom,
and from his mouth come
knowledge and understanding.

He holds victory in store for the upright,
he is a shield to those whose walk is
blameless,

for he guards the course of the just
and protects the way of his faithful ones.

Then you will understand what is right and just
and fair—every good path.

For wisdom will enter your heart,
and knowledge will be pleasant to your soul.

Discretion will protect you,
and understanding will guard you.

Wisdom will save you from the ways
    of wicked men,
from men whose words are perverse,

who leave the straight paths
to walk in dark ways,

who delight in doing wrong
and rejoice in the perverseness of evil,

whose paths are crooked
and who are devious in their ways.

It will save you also from the adulteress,
from the wayward wife with her
        seductive words,

who has left the partner of her youth
and ignored the covenant she made
        before God.

For her house leads down to death
and her paths to the spirits of the dead.

None who go to her return
or attain the paths of life.

Thus you will walk in the ways of good men
and keep to the paths of the righteous.

For the upright will live in the land,
and the blameless will remain in it;

but the wicked will be cut off from the land,
and the unfaithful will be torn from it.

Proverbs 2:1-22 NIV

Prayer

Father, I thank You for filling me with Your Spirit, giving me great wisdom, ability, and skill in accomplishing the work to which You have called me.

Thank You for imparting to me wisdom and understanding to know how to carry out all the work of establishing and building _____ (name of firm). My mouth shall speak of wisdom, and the meditation of my heart shall be of understanding.

I thank You that I am in Christ Jesus, who has become for me wisdom from You—that is, my righteousness, holiness, and redemption. I am filled with the knowledge of Your will through all spiritual wisdom and understanding, that I may live a life worthy of You and may please You in every way: bearing fruit in every good work, growing in the knowledge of You.

In Jesus' name I pray, amen.

Scripture References

Exodus 31:3 TLB

1 Corinthians 1:30 NIV

Exodus 36:1

Colossians 1:9,10 NIV

Psalm 49:3

"Issues of life and death can be decided upon only by people who are willing to do their homework and develop their insights and opinions through seeking God's kingdom."

MIKE SINGLETARY

Walking in God's Perfect Will

Lord and God, You are worthy to receive glory and honor and power, for You created all things; by Your will they were created and have their being. You adopted me as Your child through Jesus Christ, in accordance with Your pleasure and will. I pray that I may be active in sharing my faith, so that I will have a full understanding of every good thing I have in Christ.

Father, I ask You to give me a complete understanding of what You want to do in my life, and I ask You to make me wise with spiritual wisdom. Then the way I live will always honor and please You, and I will continually do good, kind things for others. All the while, I will learn to know You better and better.

Jesus has been made unto me wisdom. I single-mindedly walk in that wisdom, expecting to know what to do in every situation and to be on top of every circumstance!

I roll my works upon You [commit and trust them wholly to You: and You cause my thoughts to become agreeable to Your will, [and] so my plans are established and succeed. You direct my steps and make them sure. I understand and firmly grasp what Your will is, for I am not vague, thoughtless, and foolish. I stand firm and mature [in spiritual growth], convinced and fully assured in everything willed by You.

Father, You have destined and appointed me to come progressively to know Your will [to perceive, to recognize more strongly and clearly and to become better and more intimately acquainted with Your will].

I thank You, Father, for the Holy Spirit, who abides [permanently] in me and guides me into all truth (the whole, full truth) and speaks whatever He hears from You and announces and declares to me the things that are to come. I have the mind of Christ and do hold the thoughts (feelings and purposes) of His heart.

So, Father, I have entered into Your blessed rest by believing (trusting in, clinging to, and relying on) You.

Hallelujah!

In Jesus' name I pray, amen.

Scripture References

Philemon 6

Colossians 4:12 AMP

John 10:27

Acts 22:14 AMP

John 10:5

1 John 2:20,27 AMP

Colossians 1:9,10 AMP

John 16:13 AMP

1 Corinthians 1:30

1 Corinthians 2:16 AMP

James 1:5-8

Hebrews 4:10 AMP

Proverbs 16:3,9 AMP

John 3:16 AMP

Ephesians 5:17 AMP

Proverbs 3:5,6

Psalm 119:105

John 14:26

Joshua 1:8

James 1:22

"No people can be bound to acknowledge and adore the invisible Hand which conducts the affairs of men more than those of the United States."

GEORGE WASHINGTON

Trusting in God

Devotional Reading

For all God's words are right, and everything he does is worthy of our trust. He loves whatever is just and good; the earth is filled with his tender love. He merely spoke, and the heavens were formed, and all the galaxies of stars. He made the oceans, pouring them into his vast reservoirs.

Let everyone in all the world—men, women and children—fear the Lord and stand in awe of him. For when he but spoke, the world began! It appeared at his command! And with a breath he can scatter the plans of all the nations who oppose him, but his own plan stands forever. His intentions are the same for every generation.

Psalm 33:4-11 TLB

Prayer

Father, I ask for grace to trust You more. When I feel afraid I will trust in You. I praise Your Word. My God, in You I trust; I am not afraid. What can mortal man do to me?

Lord, Your steadfast love never ceases, Your mercies never come to an end; they are new every morning; great is Your faithfulness. You are my portion; therefore, I will hope in You.

May You, the God of hope, fill me with all joy and peace as I trust in You, so that I may overflow with hope by the power of the Holy Spirit.

To You, O Lord, I pray, and according to Your Word You will not fail me, for I am trusting You. None who has faith in You, Father, will ever be disgraced for trusting You.

Show me the path where I should go, O Lord; point out the right road for me to walk. Lead me; teach me; for You are the God who gives me salvation.

Lord, I have no fear of bad news; my heart is steadfast, trusting in You. My heart is secure; I will have no fear.

Because You are faithful and trustworthy, I make a commitment to trust in You with all my heart and lean not on my own understanding; in all my ways I acknowledge You, and You will make my paths straight. I am blessed, for I trust in the Lord, in whom is my confidence.

In Jesus' name I pray, amen.

Scripture References

Psalm 56:3,4 NIV

Psalm 112:7,8 NIV

Lamentations 3:22-24 RSV

Proverbs 3:5,6 NIV

Romans 15:13 NIV

Jeremiah 17:7 NIV

Psalm 25:1-5 TLB

"It is in the man of piety and inward principle, that we may expect to find the uncorrupted patriot, the useful citizen, and the invincible soldier."

REV. JOHN WITHERSPOON

PRESIDENT OF PRINCETON UNIVERSITY

SIGNER OF THE DECLARATION
OF INDEPENDENCE

Using Discretion

Devotional Reading

Praise the Lord.

Blessed is the man who fears the Lord,

Who greatly delights in his commandments!

His descendants will be mighty in the land;

The generation of the upright will
be blessed.

Wealth and riches are in his house;

And his righteousness endures for ever.

Light rises in the darkness for the upright;

The Lord is gracious, merciful, and
righteous.

It is well with the man who deals generously
and lends,

who conducts his affairs with justice.

For the righteous will never be moved;

he will be remembered for ever.

He is not afraid of evil tidings;

his heart is firm, trusting in the Lord.

His heart is steady, he will not be afraid,

until he sees his desire on his adversaries.

He has distributed freely, he has given to the
poor;

his righteousness endures for ever;

his horn is exalted in honor.

The wicked man sees it and is angry;

he gnashes his teeth and melts away;

the desire of the wicked man comes to
nought.

Psalm 112:1-10 RSV

Prayer

Father, I thank You for the virtue of discretion.

You give me knowledge and discretion. Discretion
protects me, and understanding guards me.

I preserve sound judgment and discernment; I will not let
them out of my sight; they will be life for me, and an orna-
ment to grace my neck. Then I will go on my way in safety,
and my foot will not stumble; when I lie down, I will not be
afraid; when I lie down, my sleep will be sweet. I have no
fear of sudden disaster or of the ruin that overtakes the
wicked, for You, Lord, will be my confidence and will keep
my foot from being snared.

Father, I pay attention to Your wisdom, and listen well to
Your words of insight, that I may maintain discretion and my
lips may preserve knowledge. Godly discretion defers anger
and gives me patience; it enables me to overlook an offense.

Father, You are my God and my Teacher; You instruct
me in discretion.

All this comes from You, the Lord Almighty. You are wonderful in counsel and magnificent in wisdom. Praise the Lord!

In Jesus' name I pray, amen.

Scripture References

Proverbs 1:4	Proverbs 19:11
Proverbs 2:11 NIV	Proverbs 19:11 NIV
Proverbs 3:21-26 NIV	Isaiah 28:26
Proverbs 5:1,2 NIV	Isaiah 28:29 NIV

"The church was and is the foundation of our community. It became our strength, our refuge, and our haven."

ROSA PARKS

Displaying Integrity

Father, when You test my heart, may You be pleased with my honesty. In everything I do may I set an example by doing what is good.

In my place of business may I show integrity, seriousness, and soundness of speech that cannot be condemned, so that those who oppose me may be ashamed because they have nothing bad to say about me. I purpose to manage, as David did, with integrity of heart; with skillful hands he led the people.

Father, I thank You that the integrity of the upright guides me. May I be blameless in Your sight so that I will receive a good inheritance. Let it be said of me by all individuals, "We know you are a person of integrity and that you teach the way of God in accordance with the truth."

Judge me, O Lord, according to my righteousness, according to my integrity, O Most High, and make me secure and guard me in Your righteousness. In my integrity You uphold me and set me in Your presence forever.

In Jesus' name I pray, amen.

Scripture References

1 Chronicles 29:17 NIV	Matthew 22:16 NIV
Titus 2:7,8 NIV	Psalm 7:8 NIV
Psalm 78:12 NIV	Proverbs 13:5 NIV

Proverbs 11:3 NIV   Psalm 41:12 NIV

Proverbs 28:10 NIV

"People with humility don't think less of themselves, they just think of themselves less."

KEN BLANCHARD

Exercising Humility

Devotional Reading

If you have any encouragement from being united
with Christ, if any comfort from his love, if any fellowship
with the Spirit, if any tenderness and compassion, then
make my joy complete by being like-minded, having the
same love, being one in spirit and purpose. Do nothing
out of selfish ambition or vain conceit, but in humility
consider others better than yourselves. Each of you should
look not only to your own interests, but also to the interests of others.

Your attitude should be the same as that of Christ
Jesus: who, being in very nature God, did not consider
equality with God something to be grasped, but made
himself nothing, taking the very nature of a servant, being
made in human likeness. And being found in appearance
as a man, he humbled himself and became obedient to
death—even death on a cross! Therefore God exalted him
to the highest place and gave him the name that is above
every name, that at the name of Jesus every knee should
bow, in heaven and on earth and under the earth, and
every tongue confess that Jesus Christ is Lord, to the glory
of God the Father.

Philippians 2:1-11 NIV

Prayer

Father, I choose to clothe myself in humility and to
receive Your grace as I humble myself before Your mighty

hand. I expect a life of victory and awesome deeds because my actions are done on behalf of a spirit humbly submitted to Your truth and righteousness.

Allow my thoughts and actions to be pure, just, and right. May I adjust my life so that I will know and understand the surety of Your plan for me.

Father, allow me to test my own actions, so that I can have appropriate self-esteem without comparing myself to somebody else. The security of Your guidance will allow me to carry my own load with energy and confidence.

I desire to listen carefully and hear what is being said to me. I incline my ear to wisdom and apply my heart to understanding and insight.

Father, I know and confess that humility and the fear of the Lord bring wealth and honor and life. Therefore, as one of Your chosen people, holy and dearly loved, I clothe myself with compassion, kindness, humility, gentleness, and patience. I bear with others and forgive whatever grievances I may have against anyone. I forgive as You forgave me. And over all these virtues I put on love, which binds them all together in perfect unity. I let the peace of Christ rule in my heart, and I am thankful.

Father, may Your will be done on earth in my life as it is in heaven. In Jesus' name, I pray. Amen.

Scripture References

1 Peter 5:5 NIV

Psalm 45:4 NIV

Galatians 6:4,5 NIV

Proverbs 18:12,13 NIV

Proverbs 2:2

Proverbs 22:4 NIV

Colossians 3:12-15 NIV

Matthew 6:10 NIV

To Watch What You Say

Father, I commit to turn from idle words and foolishly talking about things that are contrary to my true desire for myself and others. Your Word says that the tongue defiles, that it sets on fire the course of nature, that it is set on fire of hell. My words have the power to change the course of history.

In the name of Jesus, I am determined to take control of my tongue. I am determined that hell will not set my tongue on fire. I renounce, reject, and repent of every word that has ever proceeded out of my mouth against You, Lord, and Your kingdom, and against others. I cancel the power of those evil words and dedicate my mouth to speak excellent things and right things. My mouth shall utter truth.

Father, I attend to Your words; I consent and submit to Your sayings. I will not let them depart from my sight; I keep them in the center of my heart, for they are life to me and to those to whom I speak—healing and health to all our flesh. I keep and guard my heart with all vigilance and above all that I guard, for out of it flow the springs of life. I put away from me false and dishonest speech, and willful and contrary talk I put far from me. My eyes look right on [with fixed purpose], and my gaze is straight before me. I guard my mouth and my heart with all diligence. I refuse to give Satan any place in me.

Father, Your Word is a top priority to me. Your words are spirit and life. I let Your Word dwell in me richly in all wisdom. Your ability is released within me by the words of my mouth; therefore, I speak forth Your words. They are alive and working in me because You are alive and working in me. So I can boldly say that my words are words of faith, words of power, words of love, and words of life.

My words produce good things in my life and in the lives of others because I choose Your words for my lips, I choose Your will for my life, and I go forth in the power of those words to perform them in Jesus' name. Amen.

Scripture References

Matthew 12:36	Proverbs 4:20-25 AMP
Ephesians 5:4	Proverbs 21:23
2 Timothy 2:16	Ephesians 4:27
James 3:6	John 6:63
Proverbs 8:6,7	Colossians 3:16

Walking in Peace

Father, I will guard my heart; and Your peace, which transcends all understanding, will guard my heart and mind. I am the custodian of my thoughts, and I cast down every imagination that would lead to weariness, disappointment, and defeat. I am free to think on good things.

Because I love life and desire to see many good days, I keep my tongue from evil and my lips from speaking lies. I turn from evil and do good; I seek peace and pursue it. In my heart I have planned my course, and I look to You, Lord, to determine my steps.

I keep myself free from selfish ambition and the love of money. I am content with what I have because You have said, "Never will I leave you; never will I forsake you." So I say with confidence, "The Lord is my Helper; I will not be afraid. What can man do to me?"

Surely goodness and mercy shall follow me today and all the days of my life, in the name of Jesus. I write mercy and truth upon the tablets of my heart, and You will cause me to find favor and good understanding with mankind.

I shall go out before cameras and live audiences in joy, and I will be led forth in peace. I will not be anxious about what I have to speak or what I am to say; for what I am to say will be given to me in that hour; for it is not I who speaks, but the Spirit of my Father speaking through me.

Lord, Your peace will act as umpire [continually] in my heart and will settle with finality all my decisions. You will keep me in perfect peace, Father, for my mind is stayed on You. In Jesus' name I pray, amen.

Scripture References

Proverbs 4:23 NIV

Philippians 4:7,8 NIV

Psalm 34:12-14 NIV

Proverbs 16:9 NIV

Isaiah 26:3

Hebrews 13:5,6 NIV

Psalm 23:6

Colossians 3:15 AMP

Isaiah 55:12

Matthew 10:19,20

Section II

PERSONAL PRAYERS FOR GOVERNMENT LEADERS

I exhort therefore, that, first of all,
supplications, prayers, intercessions, and
giving of thanks, be made for all men; For
kings, and for all that are in authority; that
we may lead a quiet and peaceable life in all
godliness and honesty.

First Timothy 2:1,2

Introduction

We need a spiritual revolution in our world. Our country is in great need of a spiritual revolution, and it will take government, church, and business leaders working together to reverse the downward spiral we are on. Never at any time in our history has division been more obvious. Jesus said, "A house divided against itself cannot stand."

"One nation, under God, indivisible, with liberty and justice for all," we intoned as we stood with our hands over our hearts. A nation we thought indivisible, but today we are at a crossroads. Will we take the high road or the low road?

I remember when we honored the office of the president of our country whether or not we agreed with their politics. The person in the White House was our president, and we were honored to be Americans. We were grateful to live in the land of the free and the home of the brave. We had self-respect, and we respected others even when we disagreed. We were not out to smear another person. We discussed political issues and the best way to fulfill the vision for our country as stated in the Pledge of Allegiance.

Where are the God-fearing men and women who are willing to set personal agendas aside and work for righteousness and the good of the people? Are you seeking power and fame, or are you seeking to do the will of God for a nation that has been so blessed by Him?

The Old Testament prophet, Daniel, was a man of prayer who knew the God who removes and sets up government leaders. He wrote, "Blessed be the name of God forever and ever! For wisdom and might are His! He changes the times and the seasons; He removes kings and sets up kings. He gives wisdom to the wise and knowledge to those who have understanding! He reveals the deep and secret things; He knows what is in the darkness, and the light dwells with Him! I thank You and praise You, O God of my fathers, who has given me wisdom and might and has made known to me now what we desired of You, for You have made known to us the solution to the king's problem."[1]

When God singles you out as a leader, He empowers you with the ability to fulfill His purposes. His ability is His divine power giving you everything you need for life and godliness through your knowledge of Him who called you to serve others.

The prayers in this section will help you to remain focused on God, who has all the answers and gives you wisdom and insight to the enigmas of our society and government.

---

[1] Daniel 2:21-23

Maintaining My Relationship with God

Father, except Your presence go with me I shall not go. Leading a nation is an awesome, fearful place of responsibility, and I need to be strong, alert, and courageous to Your Spirit, and work heartily at my tasks as unto You, my Lord. Holy Spirit, keep me alert to Your promptings as You bring all things to my remembrance that I must know to fulfill God's plan and purposes.

Fellowship and communion with You, my Father, will remain my top priority because I love You with my entire being; spirit, soul (mind), and body. I delight myself in You, my Lord, so that I might remain flexible, openhearted, and tender for obedience. Thank You for directing my steps and ordering my conversation aright.

You are my God and I will praise You continually.

Adapted from *The Prayer Saturated Church*
by Cheryl Sacks

Scripture References

Exodus 33:15   Jeremiah 29:11

Matthew 22:37   Psalm 37:4

Psalm 50:23

Keeping Priorities in Check

Father, in the name of Jesus, I ask for discernment to know and understand the priorities as You have given them to me. I ask for Your wisdom to know how to appropriate my time. As I prepare for bed I realize there is so very much that needs attention. When I arise there are already situations that need to be addressed. I ask You for the needed wisdom and strength to complete my appointed tasks. You are the strength of my life—You are my light and my salvation. Father, You are at work in me and energizing me both to will and work for Your good pleasure, satisfaction, and delight.

Scripture References

Proverbs 3:5,6   James 1:7

Psalm 27:1   Philippians 2:13

Staying Healthy

Father, I choose to give attention to Your words and incline my ear to Your sayings. I keep them before my eyes and in the midst of my heart, for they are life to me and health to all my flesh. I keep my heart with all diligence, for out of it spring the issues of life. I put away from myself a deceitful mouth and put perverse lips far from me. My eyes look straight ahead, and my eyelids look right before You. I ponder the path of my feet, and all my ways are established. I will not turn to the right or to the left. I shall prosper and be in health even as my soul prospers.

Scripture References

Proverbs 4:20-26   3 John 2

"In regard to this Great Book, I have but to say, it is the best gift God has given to man. All the good the Savior gave to the world was communicated through this book."

ABRAHAM LINCOLN

Reinforcing America's Vision

Father, in the name of Jesus, I come into Your presence thanking You for this nation that You ordained for Your purposes.

You have called me to be Your representative in this city/state/nation where I live and around the world. Father, I believe that You have called me to maintain the intent and purposes of our founding fathers and to uphold the Constitution as it was written that freedom might continue—not the freedom to violate divine laws but the freedom to do what's right. Our children are often violated, the poor are maligned, flags are burned, and crimes are excused in the name of freedom of speech. Lord, this should not be!

First, I recognize that You are God and everything was made by and for You. Secondly, I am a servant of Jesus Christ, called to act as Your representative in a government role and fulfill Your purposes and plans for this great nation. I seek Your wisdom to do that which pleases You—to do what is right rather than what is popular. Holy Spirit, I devote myself to attending to the services of this great nation, knowing that You are my Divine Helper.

A house divided against itself cannot stand. I know that You have a plan that will unite us, and I ask for wisdom that surpasses the wisdom of all those who oppose righteousness.

Even though we may have differing ideas about how to perform Your will, I pray we will be united in purpose.

Without a vision this nation will perish. Grant unto me, Your representative, a boldness to speak truth for this people. I thank You for sending wise counselors, public servants, military attaché, cultural attaché, and diplomats for every manner of work in our government and around the world. I proclaim that each department is operating in the excellence of ministry. You give wisdom and ability to each office of the government for the edifying of this nation.

I ask for Your wisdom to fulfill Your plan to bring the people into harmony, establishing a nation of people who support and honor one another, a nation that is committed to raising the poor from the dust and lifting the needy from the ash heap.

We are a nation that blesses Israel, and we are blessed. You created mankind with a free will, and You desire that we use our freedom to do righteous deeds—we assume our responsibility to be a light to the nations. I ask for Your wisdom as I speak to the people and encourage them to lay aside selfish agendas.

Our nation is a republic, one nation under God, prospering financially, and we have more than enough to meet every situation. We have everything we need to carry out Your Great Commission.

We declare that Jesus is Lord over the people of our great nation! Amen.

Scripture References

Acts 4:24	Ephesians 4:11-15
Romans 4:17	Philippians 4:19
1 Corinthians 1:10	Romans 5:5
Acts 4:29	1 Corinthians 3:9
Mark 16:20	Psalm 63:4
Exodus 35:33	Psalm 113:7

"From Jesus Christ's leadership model we learn that leadership is about serving first. Then, from the position of serving others, the leader guides others toward a vision.... What an alienated, hurting, and divided world needs is more servant leaders."

DR. BARBARA WILLIAMS-SKINNER

Adopting an Attitude of Humility

Father, in the name of Jesus I renounce egotism and put off wrong attitudes and sins that would so easily beset me and frustrate my goals and Your purposes. I choose humility—a humble attitude—not thinking of myself more highly than I should.

First of all I seek Your way of doing and being right. I will remain teachable, knowing that as I commit my way unto You that You will cause my thoughts to be agreeable to Your will, and my plans shall be established and succeed.

Holy Spirit, I ask You to help me as I test my own actions and develop appropriate self-esteem, without comparing myself to anyone. Help me to focus on issues and to have no need to smear another's reputation. The security of Your guidance allows me to carry my own load with energy and confidence.

Give me the patience to listen carefully and hear what is being said. Today, in every situation I incline my ear to wisdom and apply my heart to understanding and insight. Father, I submit to Your leadership. When You called me, You also equipped me, and I have applied myself to develop my talents and abilities through education in every area of my life.

Today, I bind my mind and attitude to compassion, kindness, humility, gentleness, and patience. I bear with others and forgive whatever grievances I may have against anyone. I forgive as You forgave me. And over all these virtues I put on love, which binds them all together in perfect harmony. The peace of God shall rule in my heart, and I have an attitude of gratitude, knowing it is not in my own strength, might, or power but by Your Spirit that I am successful in all that I do and hope to achieve in the name of Jesus.

May my work be beneficial to my co-workers and the people of this nation and bring glory to Your name, O Most High! Amen.

Scripture References

Proverbs 16:3	1 Peter 5:5
Matthew 6:33	Psalm 45:1,4
Proverbs 22:4	Galatians 6:4,5
Colossians 3:12-15	Hebrews 12:1

"No greater thing could come to our land today than revival of the spirit of faith—a revival that would sweep through the homes of the nation and stir the hearts of men and women of all faiths to a reassertion of their belief in God and their dedication to His will for themselves and for their world. I doubt if there is any problem—social, political or economic—that would not melt away before the fires of such spiritual revival."

FRANKLIN DELANO ROOSEVELT

Our Citizens

Father, in the name of Jesus I pray for the people of this great nation. I forgive those who have turned their backs on our history, even declaring themselves atheists. It is my prayer that Your Word will run swiftly throughout every city and village of this country.

Holy Spirit, I thank You for giving me a spirit of counsel and wisdom so that I may communicate a message of hope for this country. You give the wise answer and I pray that my words will be a demonstration of Your wisdom operating in me, stirring in the hearts of my hearers the most holy emotions and thus persuading them that Your will must be done if this nation is to survive and fulfill its destiny.

Father, thank You for hearing my prayers and moving by Your Spirit in our land. There are famines, earthquakes, floods, natural disasters, and violence occurring. Men's hearts are failing them because of fear. May Your people recognize the need for spiritual revolution in this nation and be shining beacons of light to the world.

Jesus, You spoke of discerning the signs of the times. Give the people of this nation a spirit of wisdom and revelation, that they will watch and pray.

Search us, O God, and know our hearts; try us, and know our thoughts today. See if there be any wicked way in us, and lead us in the way everlasting. Forgive us our sins of judging inappropriately, complaining about and criticizing our leaders. Cleanse us with hyssop, and we will be clean; wash us, and we will be whiter than snow. Touch our lips with coals from Your altar that we may pray prayers that avail much for all men and women everywhere.

Lord, we desire to release rivers of living water for the healing of the nations in the name of Jesus. Amen.

Scripture References

Luke 21:11,25,26	Psalm 51:7 NIV
Matthew 16:3	Isaiah 6:6,7 NIV
Matthew 26:41	James 5:16
James 4:10	1 Timothy 2:1
1 Peter 3:4	John 7:38
Matthew 5:5	Revelation 22:1,2
Psalm 139:23	

"I now make it my earnest prayer that God would have you and the State over which you preside in His holy protection, that He would incline the hearts of the citizens to cultivate a spirit of subordination and obedience to government, to entertain a brotherly affection and a love for one another—for their fellow citizens of the United States at large, and particularly for their brethren who have served in the field—and finally, that He would most graciously be pleased to dispose us all to do justice, to love mercy, and to demean ourselves with that charity, humility, and {peaceful} temper of the mind which were the characteristics of the Divine Author of our blessed religion, without a humble imitation of whose example in these things, we can hope to be a happy nation."

GEORGE WASHINGTON

(CLOSING PRAYER FROM A LETTER SENT TO THE THIRTEEN GOVERNORS AND STATE LEGISLATOR UPON HIS RESIGNATION AS COMMANDER-IN-CHIEF)

Our Government

Father, in Jesus' name, we give thanks for the United States and its government. I pray and intercede for every official: the president, the representatives, the senators, the judges of our land, the policemen and the policewomen, the governors and mayors, and for all those who are in authority in any way. We pray that the Spirit of the Lord rests upon each one.

In the name of Jesus I decree that skillful and godly wisdom has entered into the heart of each government official, and knowledge is pleasant to us. Discretion watches over us; understanding keeps us and delivers us from the way of evil and from evil men.

Father, I ask that You compass Your appointed government officials with counselors like Joseph of old. I pray our hearts and ears will be attentive to godly counsel, and we will do that which is right in Your sight. May we be men and women of integrity who are obedient concerning the people of this country, that we may lead a quiet and peaceable life in all godliness and honesty.

Father, there is no authority except that which You have established. The authorities that exist have been established by You. As a nation, we pray that the upright shall dwell in our government—that men and women who are blameless and complete in Your sight shall remain in these positions of authority, but the wicked shall be cut off from our government and the treacherous shall be rooted out of it.

Your Word declares that blessed is the nation whose God is the Lord. I receive Your blessing for these people. Father, You are their refuge and stronghold in times of trouble (high cost, destitution, and desperation). So I declare with my mouth that Your people dwell safely in this land, and we will prosper abundantly so that we may be a blessing to other nations. We are more than conquerors through Christ Jesus!

It is written in Your Word that the heart of the king is in the hand of the Lord, and You turn it whichever way You desire. I declare that our hearts are in Your hand and our decisions are divinely directed of You.

We give thanks unto You, Father, that the good news of the Gospel is published in our land. The Word of the Lord prevails and grows mightily in the hearts and lives of the people. We give thanks for this land and the leaders You have given to us, in Jesus' name.

Jesus is Lord over the United States! Amen.

Scripture References

1 Timothy 2:1-3	Deuteronomy 28:10,11
Proverbs 2:10-12,21,22	Romans 8:37 AMP
Psalm 33:12	Proverbs 21:1
Psalm 9:9	Acts 12:24
Psalm 33:12	

"Be willing to make decisions.
That's the most important quality in a
good leader."

GENERAL GEORGE S. PATTON JR.

"Leadership is a combination of
strategy and character. If you must be
without one, be without the strategy."

GENERAL H. NORMAN SCHWARZKOPF

Our Military

Father, our troops have been sent into _____ as peacekeepers. We petition You, Lord, according to Psalm 91, for the safety of our military personnel.

This is no afternoon athletic contest that our armed forces will walk away from and forget about in a couple of hours. This is for keeps, a life-or-death fight to the finish against the devil and all his demons. We look beyond human instruments of conflict and address the forces and authorities and rulers of darkness and powers in the spiritual world.

As children of the Most High God, we enforce the triumphant victory of our Lord Jesus Christ. Our Lord stripped principalities and powers, making a show of them openly. Thank You, Jesus, for defeating the evil one and his forces of darkness and giving us authority over them in Your name, the name that is above every name. All power and authority both in heaven and earth belong to You. Righteousness and truth shall prevail, and nations shall come to the light of the Gospel.

We petition heaven to turn our troops into a real peace-keeping force by pouring out the glory of God through our men and women in that part of the world. Use them as instruments of righteousness to defeat the plans of the devil.

Lord, we plead the power of the blood of Jesus, asking You to manifest Your power and glory. We entreat You on behalf of the citizens in these countries on both sides of this conflict. They have experienced pain and heartache. They are victims of the devil's strategies to steal, kill, and destroy. We pray that they will come to know Jesus, who came to give us life and life more abundantly.

We stand in the gap for the people of the war-torn land. We expect an overflowing of Your goodness and glory in the lives of those for whom we are praying. May they call upon Your name and be saved.

Lord, You make known Your salvation. Your righteousness You openly show in the sight of the nations.

Father, provide for and protect the families of our armed forces. Preserve marriages, cause the hearts of the parents to turn toward their children and the hearts of the children to turn toward their fathers and mothers. We plead the blood of Jesus over our troops and their families.

Provide a support system to undergird, uplift, and edify those who have been left to raise children by themselves. Jesus has been made unto these parents wisdom, righteousness, and sanctification. Through Your Holy Spirit, comfort the lonely and strengthen the weary.

Father, we are looking forward to that day when the whole earth shall be filled with the knowledge of the Lord as the waters cover the sea. In Jesus' name, amen.

A portion of this prayer was taken from a letter dated January 22, 1996, written by Kenneth Copeland of Kenneth Copeland Ministries in Fort Worth, Texas, and sent to his partners. Used by permission.

Scripture References

Ephesians 6:12 THE MESSAGE

Colossians 2:15

John 10:10

Ezekiel 22:30

Acts 2:21

Psalm 98:2 AMP

Malachi 4:6

1 Corinthians 1:30

Isaiah 11:9

"The Americans combine the notions of Christianity and of liberty so intimately in their minds, that it is impossible to make them conceive the one without the other.... [They have] an ostensible respect for Christian morality and virtue... [and] almost all education is entrusted to the clergy."

ALEXIS DE TOCQUEVILLE

Our Schools

Father, we thank You that the entrance of Your Word brings light and that You watch over Your Word to perform it. Now we bring before You the _____ school system(s) and the men and women who are in positions of authority within our schools. We ask You to give them skillful and godly wisdom, that Your knowledge might be pleasant to them. Then discretion will watch over them, and understanding will keep them and deliver them from the way of evil and from evil men.

We pray that men and women of integrity, blameless and complete in Your sight, remain in teaching, counseling, and administrative positions, but that the wicked be cut off and the treacherous be rooted out in the name of Jesus. Father, we thank You for born-again, Spirit-filled people in these positions.

Father, we bring our children and young people before You. We speak forth Your Word boldly and confidently, that we and our households are saved in the name of Jesus. We are redeemed from the curse of the law, for Jesus was made a curse for us. Our sons and daughters are not given to another people. We enjoy our children, and they shall not go into the captivity of the world's thinking and ways, in the name of Jesus.

As parents we train our children in the way they should go, and when they are old they shall not depart from it. Our children shrink from whatever might offend You or discredit the name of Christ. They show themselves to be blameless, guileless, innocent, and uncontaminated children of God, without blemish (faultless, unrebukable), in the midst of a crooked and wicked generation, holding out to it and offering to all the Word of Life. Thank You, Father, that You give them knowledge and skill in all learning and wisdom and bring them into favor with those around them.

We pray and intercede that these young people, their parents, and the leaders in the school system(s) separate themselves from contact with contaminating and corrupting influences and cleanse themselves from everything that would contaminate and defile their spirits, souls, and bodies. We confess that they shun immorality and all sexual looseness—flee from impurity in thought, word, or deed—and they live and conduct themselves honorably and becomingly as in the open light of day. We confess and believe that they shun youthful lusts and flee from them in the name of Jesus.

Father, we ask You to commission the ministering spirits to go forth and police all school properties, dispelling the forces of darkness.

We thank You that in Christ all the treasures of divine wisdom (of comprehensive insight into the ways and purposes of God) and all the riches of spiritual knowledge and enlightenment are stored up and lie hidden for us, and we walk in Him.

Praise You, Father, that we shall see the children of this nation walking in the ways of piety and virtue, revering Your name, Father. Those who err in spirit will come to understanding, and those who murmur discontentedly will accept instruction in the way, Jesus, to Your will, and carry out Your purposes in their lives; for You, Father, occupy first place in their hearts. We surround our nation's children with our faith.

Thank You, Father, that You are the delivering God. Thank You that the good news of the Gospel is published throughout our school system(s). Thank You for intercessors to stand on Your Word and for laborers of the harvest to preach Your Word in Jesus' name. Praise the Lord! Amen.

Scripture References

Psalm 119:130	2 Timothy 2:21 AMP
Jeremiah 1:12	2 Corinthians 7:1 AMP
Proverbs 2:10-12 AMP	1 Corinthians 6:18 AMP
Proverbs 2:21,22 AMP	Romans 13:13 AMP
Acts 16:31	Ephesians 5:4
Galatians 3:13	2 Timothy 2:22
Deuteronomy 28:32,41	Matthew 18:18
Proverbs 22:6 AMP	2 Timothy 2:26
Philippians 2:15,16 AMP	Hebrews 1:14
Daniel 1:17 AMP	Colossians 2:3 AMP
Daniel 1:9	Isaiah 29:23,24 AMP
1 John 2:16,17 AMP	

Pleasing God Rather Than Man

Father, I desire to please You rather than men. Forgive me for loving the approval and the praise and the glory that come from men [instead of and] more than the glory that comes from You. [I value my credit with You more than credit with men.]

I declare that I am free from the fear of man, which brings a snare. I lean on, trust in, and put my confidence in You. I am safe and set on high. I take comfort and am encouraged and confidently and boldly say, "The Lord is my Helper; I will not be seized with alarm [I will not fear or dread or be terrified]. What can man do to me?"

Just as You sent Jesus, You have sent me. You are ever with me, for I always seek to do what pleases You. In Jesus' name I pray, amen.

Scripture References

John 12:43 AMP	John 17:18 AMP
Proverbs 29:25 AMP	John 8:29 AMP
Hebrews 13:6 AMP	

"I know how embarrassing this matter is to politicians, bureaucrats, businessmen, and cynics; but, whatever these honored men think, the irrefutable truth is that the soul of America is at its best and highest, Christian."

CHARLES HABIB MALIK (1906-1967)

LEBANON'S AMBASSADOR TO
THE UNITED NATIONS

Honoring God in Governmental Issues

Defining Honor

Honor denotes a fine sense of and a strict conformity to what is considered morally right or due: honesty, fairness, or integrity in one's beliefs and actions. Honor, honesty, integrity, and sincerity refer to the highest moral principles and the absence of deceit or fraud.

Prayer

Father, You have called me, anointed me, and appointed me to work as Your representative. I pray that I will always walk worthy of this calling, that I might honor You in every discussion and in every situation. I am singled-minded, determined never to compromise my core belief in You and Your Truth.

With the help of the Holy Spirit I choose to keep all Your commandments, and You will establish me in the work You have called me to do.

I thank You that Your presence will go with me, and in the day of trouble You will hear my call and You will deliver me. You will establish me and teach me Your way, so that I may walk and live in Your truth. I ask You to direct and unite my heart so that I always fear and honor Your name.

Today and every day Lord, I desire that You grant me the wisdom and knowledge to make decisions that are in keeping

with Your Word and that will be beneficial to me and each
person I encounter.

Each day, Lord, help me to walk as an honorable servant
of Jesus Christ of Nazareth and display the light of the
kingdom in every place I am called to be.

Amen.

Scripture References

Psalm 4:3 AMP   Psalm 50:15 AMP

Psalm 86:11 AMP   Matthew 5:16 AMP

"It is alleged by men of loose principles, or defective views of the subject, that religion and morality are not necessary or important qualifications for political stations. But the Scriptures teach a different doctrine. They direct that rulers should be men who rule in the fear of God, able men, such as fear God, men of truth, hating covetousness."

NOAH WEBSTER

Acting with Integrity

Father, when You test my heart, may You be pleased with my honesty. In everything I do, may I set an example by doing what is right. I will keep my word and "swear to my own hurt" regardless of the cost.

In my governmental position help me to always show integrity, seriousness, and soundness of speech that cannot be condemned, so that those who oppose me may be ashamed because they have nothing bad to say about me. I purpose to manage, as David did, with integrity of heart; with skillful hands he led the people.

The integrity of the upright shall continue to guide me. May I be blameless in Your sight so that I will receive a good inheritance. Let it be said of me by all men, "We know you are a person of integrity and that you teach the way of God in accordance with the truth."

Judge me, O Lord, according to my righteousness, according to my integrity, O Most High, and make me secure and guard me in Your righteousness. In my integrity You uphold me and set me in Your presence forever. Let integrity and uprightness preserve me; for I wait on You.

In Jesus' name I pray, amen.

Scripture References

1 Chronicles 29:17 NIV   Matthew 22:16 NIV

Titus 2:7,8 NIV   Psalm 7:8 NIV

Psalm 78:12 NIV   Proverbs 13:5 NIV

Proverbs 11:3 NIV   Psalm 41:12 NIV

Proverbs 28:10 NIV   Psalm 15:4

Psalm 25:21

Those in Need of Protection

Holy Spirit, help me pray for men and women who are on the front lines in other countries. Also, I pray for those in our own country who are called on when fires are raging out of control, those who are called into places of violence. I include all those whose lives are at risk as they work to protect the lives of others.

In the name of Jesus, I pray a hedge of protection around these men and women. I thank You, Father, that You are a wall of fire around about them, and You have sent angels to protect and defend them in all their ways of service and obedience.

May they experience Your presence in the midst of trouble. May they call upon the name of the Lord and be saved.

In Jesus' name I pray, amen.

Scripture References

Job 1:10

Zechariah 2:5

Psalm 34:7

Psalm 91:1,2

Psalm 91:4,5

Psalm 91:8-11

Psalm 91:14-16

"Being thus arrived in a good harbor, and brought safe to land, they fell upon their knees and blessed the God of Heaven who had brought them over the vast and furious ocean, and delivered them from all the perils and miseries thereof, again to set their feet on the firm and stable earth, their proper element."

WILLIAM BRADFORD

GOVERNOR OF PLYMOUTH COLONY

1621-1657

A Traveler's Prayer for Safety

Father, as I prepare to travel, I rejoice in the promises that Your Word holds for protection and safety of the righteous. Only You, Father, make me live in safety. I trust in You and dwell in Your protection. If I shall face any problems or trouble, I will run to You, Father, my strong tower and shelter in time of need. In the name of Jesus, I speak peace, safety, and success over my travel plans.

Thank You, Lord, for preserving my pathway of travel, and I am amazingly aware of the angels You have assigned to keep charge over me and surround my car/airplane/ship/train. You are faithful to deliver me from every type of evil and preserve me for Your kingdom. I am confident that my travel plans will not be disrupted or confused. Should there be any delays, show me how to use the time wisely.

No matter the mode of transportation I choose, in every situation You are there to protect me. You have redeemed me. I am Yours and You are mine. The earth and all things on it are under Your command. You are my Heavenly Father. No food or water will harm me when I arrive at my destination.

Father, I give You the glory in this situation. Your mercy is upon me, and my travels will be safe. Not a hair on my head shall perish. Thank You, Father, for Your guidance and safety. You are worthy of all praise! Amen.

Scripture References

Isaiah 55:11	Isaiah 43:1-3
Jeremiah 1:12	2 Timothy 4:18
Psalm 4:8	Hosea 2:18
Psalm 91:1	Luke 10:19
Proverbs 18:10	Psalm 91:13
Proverbs 29:25	Luke 21:18
Mark 11:23,24	Mark 16:18
Proverbs 2:8	Matthew 18:18
Psalm 91:11,12	John 14:13
2 Timothy 4:18	Daniel 9:18
Philippians 4:7	Luke 1:50
2 Timothy 1:7	

Section III

PERSONAL PRAYERS FOR SPIRITUAL LEADERS

Here are my directions: Pray much for others; plead for God's mercy upon them; give thanks for all he is going to do for them. Pray in this way for kings and all others who are in authority over us, or are in places of high responsibility, so that we can live in peace and quietness, spending our time in godly living and thinking much about the Lord.

1 Timothy 2:1,2 TLB

Introduction

Sometimes the day-to-day responsibilities of ministry can overshadow the ability to keep "the main thing as the main thing," which is our relationship with the Lord. Unless we decide to maintain a diligent pursuit of spiritual disciplines, we face the real possibility of becoming "wells without water."

In addition to protecting our personal walk and journey, we must also give space to living life with joy. It is important to take time off to have a real vacation, one not associated with a conference or sabbatical. This provides real times of rest and restoration. It is important to learn to put our name, along with our family's, on our "Top Ten Things to Do" list. Keeping our schedules in a healthy perspective and maintaining right priorities will add length to our days of service to God and His people.

The writer of Romans said, "Who shall separate us from the love of God?"[1] and we need to ask ourselves this question periodically. When we ask the Lord to teach us to pray, to teach us to walk with Him in new levels of intimacy, to teach us to slow down, and to teach us to trust Him with every aspect of our lives—we create a healthy environment in which we can experience an abundant life and add not just years to our life but life to our years.

---

[1] See Romans 8:38,39.

Several years ago I heard an interview with a pastor who was well seasoned in both years and pastoral ministry. When asked how he kept up with all the responsibilities of ministering to his large congregation and spending quality time with his family, he responded by holding up his rather well-worn Bible. His answer to the host was that the more his responsibilities increased, the more time he spent in personal prayer and study of the Word. He said it would have been impossible to consistently have a fresh word for his congregation, enjoy his family, and have the spiritual stamina to sustain himself through the years without having learned to listen for the voice of his Master.

The prayers in this section address just some of the areas that challenge those who serve as leaders in the community of faith. As you read these prayers and meditate on the attached scriptures, it is our hope that you find renewal and new strength to complete the work of the kingdom. May you decide to give more time to walking with the Shepherd and develop a new hunger to hear the voice of the Master.

"You've got to get up every morning with determination if you're going to go to bed with satisfaction."

GEORGE HORACE LORIMER

"Many people mistake our work for our vocation. Our vocation is the love of Jesus."

MOTHER TERESA

Beginning Each Day for Ministers

Father, today I place my family and ministry staff into Your keeping. You are able to keep that which I commit to You against that day. With Your help I am determined to be well-balanced (temperate, sober of mind) by casting all my cares for my family and ministry upon You.

I come before You rejoicing, for this is the day which You have made, and I choose to be glad in it. Obedience is better than sacrifice, so I choose to submit to Your will, that the plans and purposes for my life, family, and church may be conducted in a manner that will bring honor and glory to You. Cause me to be spiritually and mentally alert in this time of meditation and prayer. I tune my ear to the sound of Your voice, resisting the voice of a stranger.

With thanksgiving I acknowledge the angels that You have commanded concerning me and those who are in my charge. You sent these angels to guard us in all our ways, and they lift us up in their hands so that we will not strike our foot against a stone.

Thank You, Lord, that my associates and I continue to experience Your faithfulness to us in this ministry.

Thank You, Father, for imparting the anointing to shepherd this ministry and for your divine help and guidance. With it we can prosper and have good success in every area of the ministry. I continue to thank You for the many blessings that You have poured out upon us all.

I especially thank You for the co-laborers with whom I will be interacting today. Give me words of wisdom and words of grace, that I might encourage them and build them up. May I be alert to those who are in need of a Savior as I walk through this day.

Father, I kneel before You, from whom Your whole family in heaven and on earth derives its name. I pray that out of Your glorious riches You may strengthen each one with power through Your Spirit in the inner being, so that Christ may dwell in each heart through faith.

Now to Him who is able to do immeasurably more than all we ask or imagine, according to His power that is at work within us, to Him be the glory in Christ Jesus throughout all generations, for ever and ever!

In Jesus' name I pray. Amen.

Scripture References

Psalm 118:24	Lamentations 3:22,23
1 Samuel 15:22	Joshua 1:8
2 Timothy 1:12	Ephesians 3:14-17 NIV
Psalm 91:11,12 NIV	Ephesians 3:20 NIV

Staying Focused

Father, in the name of Jesus I come to You asking for
Your help in remaining focused on the tasks assigned to me
this day. There will be many things that come up to distract
me from what You have asked me to do. As I make decisions
on what to give attention to, help me to use wisdom. I know
that You give wisdom and out of Your mouth comes knowledge and keen discernment.

Remind me that You will be as a voice behind my ear,
saying, "This is the way. Walk in it." Help me to know that
You will always lead and guide my every step as I follow You.
I realize, Lord, that because I know Your voice, I will not
listen to the voice of strangers, who may cause me to miss
Your timing and purpose for my life. I do not have to walk in
fear or worry but will remain full of courage and strength, for
I know who abides in me. Because I have right standing with
the Father-God, I am as strong as a lion.

Father, I thank You that You keep the vision for this
church/ministry in front of me. I have written it down so
that I can follow it through to a successful end. I thank You
that from the vision You have given me, I am able to develop
a healthy and balanced schedule that will allow me to be a
good steward of my time and talents.

Father I thank You that all my steps are ordered by You,
and You lead me in the path of righteousness. I will be alert
to every good way and open door You put in my path. I say

that my heart is fixed and settled on obeying Your Word. As I follow Your lead I will experience peace and the fullness of joy that comes to those who keep their heart and mind stayed upon you. In the name of Jesus, Amen

Scripture References

Proverbs 2:6	John 10:4,5
Psalm 37:23,24	Psalm 112:7
Isaiah 30:21	Proverbs 28:1
Psalm 23:3	Isaiah 26:3
Psalm 32:8	Habakkuk 2:2
Revelation 3:7,8	

Walking in God's Love

Father, I thank You that You have shown me through Your Word that the hallmark of my life as a believer is the love that I have for the brethren. I can walk in love because the Son of Your love dwells richly in me. I can love others because You have taught me to share the love You extend to me with everyone I meet.

I pray that every day I will walk in the fullness of the characteristics of love. For love is patient, kind, without envy, not boastful, and without pride. Your love in me is not rude, self-seeking, not easily angered, and refuses to keep a record of wrongs. Your love in me will not rejoice in evil but rejoices with the truth. This love always trusts, always hopes, and always perseveres. Your love in me will never fail.

Father, I ask that my love would abound more and more in knowledge and depth of insight, so that I may be able to discern what is best and to be pure and blameless until the day of Christ. I pray that I may model this love before others in a way that will cause them to see You anew and afresh. I pray that my congregation/ministry staff will be an example of Your love in deeds, words, and behavior. I pray that we will dwell in Your love and thereby dwell continually in You. For we know that we have passed from death to life because we love the brethren.

I thank You, Lord God, that there is nothing that will be able to separate me from Your love. Nothing—not death, life, angels, demons, the present, the future, powers of any kind, heights, depths, or anything in all of creation—will stop Your love from reaching me.

I pray this in the name of Jesus. Amen.

Scripture References

1 Corinthians 13

Romans 8:38,39

1 John 3:14

Philippians 1:9,10

1 John 4:12,16

Trusting

Father, I thank You that as a pastor/ministry leader I have learned to put my trust in You for the responsibility of leading Your people. I have learned to trust You with all of my heart, and I do not lean to my own understanding. My heart is firmly fixed, trusting (leaning on and being confident) in the Lord. I know it is better to trust in You than to put my confidence in people. Each day I am given an opportunity to trust You with decisions and choices that I am called to make.

Mercy will surround me in every situation when I remember to trust You. You cause me to know the way I should walk as I continually lift my soul up before You. Help me to acknowledge You daily as my goodness, my fortress, my high tower, my deliverer, and my shield. I will not be afraid for You, Lord, are my strength and my song, and You have become my salvation. I remember that when I put my trust in You I will not be in confusion.

When anxious thoughts multiply themselves within me, Your consolations delight my soul, Lord. I pray that my life may be both a witness and an example of trust in You to those I am charged to lead and teach. Help me to teach them how to walk in the promises of the words of the Psalmist:

> The Lord is my shepherd; I shall not want. He maketh me to lie down in green pastures: he leadeth me beside the still waters. He restoreth my soul: he leadeth me in the paths of righteousness for his name's sake. Yea,

though I walk through the valley of the shadow of death, I will fear no evil: for thou art with me; thy rod and thy staff they comfort me. Thou preparest a table before me in the presence of mine enemies: thou anointest my head with oil; my cup runneth over. Surely goodness and mercy shall follow me all the days of my life: and I will dwell in the house of the Lord for ever.

Psalm 23

Scripture References

Psalm 94:19

Psalm 91:2,4,9

Psalm 5:12

Psalm 112:7

Psalm 71:1

Psalm 118: 8,9

Proverbs 3:5

Psalm 118:14

Jeremiah 42:3

"The greatest revolution of our generation is the discovery that human beings, by changing the inner attitudes of their minds, can change the outer aspects of their lives."

WILLIAM JAMES

"It would delight your heart to see how the trophies of the cross are multiplied in this institution. Yale College is a little temple: prayer and praise seem to be the delight of the greater part of the students."

BENJAMIN SILLIMAN

YALE PROFESSOR AND LECTURER 1804-1855

Keeping a Personal Prayer Time

Father, I have come to spend time with You. I have learned to seek You early. I know that if I seek You early I will find You. Before the call to things that will range from the mundane to levels of great importance, I need to satisfy my hunger for Your voice, Your counsel, and Your wisdom. There is no other way for me to keep the passion of ministry alive apart from humbling myself before You. Help me to remember the joy of fellowship with You and the comfort it brings my soul.

This discipline of prayer gives me the opportunity to recount to You my concerns, hopes, fears, and desires. It is at this time I am able to cast my cares [all my anxieties, all my worries, all my concerns, once for all] on You for You [care for me affectionately and care about me watchfully]. It affords me a place where I can sit with You and learn the rhythm of Your heart again. Our time together helps me see the larger picture of Your plans for my life. I can sit with You and talk as friend to friend. Be thou my vision forever, I pray. Amen.

(The song, *Be Thou My Vision,* can be found in Appendix C.)

Scripture References

Psalm 63:1	1 Peter 5:7
Psalm 78:34	Psalm 5:2
Proverbs 8:17	Psalm 55:17

Praising the Lord

Today and every day I will bless You, Lord, and Your praise will continually be in my mouth. I will say of You, Lord, that You are my refuge and strength and my portion forever. How lovely are Your dwelling places, my King and my God. I would rather have one day in Your courts than a thousand elsewhere. I am continuing to learn how to rest in Your precious presence and to say I hunger to be in Your courts.

Teach me to bring You praise from the rising of the sun to the going down of the same, for Your name is so worthy to be praised. Lord, who is like unto You? I say there is no one and nothing in all of creation that compares with You. I praise You for being compassionate, merciful, and full of benefits that You give to me each day.

Lord, every day I find something that causes my spirit to rejoice before Your presence. Even in times of testing and affliction my soul can magnify You. Lord, I call You the King of Glory for You alone are eternal, immortal, invisible, the all-wise God who deserves honor and glory forever and ever. Amen.

Scripture References

Psalm 34:1	Psalm 113:3,4
Psalm 94:19 NIV	Psalm 27:1
Psalm 68:19	Exodus 34:6
Psalm 84:10	1 Timothy 1:17

"A man, truly illuminated, will no more despise others than Bartimaeus, after his own eyes were opened, would take a stick and beat every blind man he met."

JOHN NEWTON (1725-1807)

(SLAVE TRADER, TURNED BELIEVER AND PASTOR, WROTE "AMAZING GRACE")

Forgiving

Father, I come to You at this time to ask forgiveness regarding the situation of _____. I come knowing that mercy and grace are available to me, and You are willing to cleanse me of unrighteousness. I desire to please You in all my ways. I realize that I was wrong and will take all the necessary steps to correct my attitude and behavior. It is impossible for me to continue fellowship with You if I have broken it with others. I will lay my gifts upon Your altar and go be reconciled with _____. Help me to speak truly and live truly before You and others, so I will not do damage to the ministry You have entrusted me with or the fellowship I have with You.

Father, I thank You for the gift of forgiveness. Thank You for cleansing my heart and renewing a right spirit within me. I know that as I make my confessions before You and renounce the sin in my life I will find You a faithful and just God. You will forgive my sin and purify me from all unrighteousness. Help me to come to You first without attempting to fix myself or the situation, because You stand ready to forgive us when we ask. I thank You that I can freely forgive others, for I desire for them to experience the same freedom that I have as You restore me to fellowship with You. Amen.

Scripture References

Hebrews 4:16   1 John 1:9

Psalm 51   Matthew 5:23

Mark. 11:25   Ephesians 4:15 AMP

Cherishing the Call

Lord, today I take time to come before You just to remember when you placed Your hand on my life, setting me apart as a minister of the Gospel of Jesus Christ. I am still awed that You would choose me to serve Your people. Thank You for the privilege I have of walking with them through all the paths of life. Help me to continue seeing each person as a unique individual created and loved by You.

I know that it is a precious thing to stand and minister before this congregation/group of believers. I thank You that Your Word remains in my heart and in my bones as a burning fire. The law of truth is in my mouth, and iniquity is not on my lips, but they keep knowledge.

Father I desire to present my body as a living sacrifice, holy and acceptable to You, which is my reasonable service. As I give my life as a vessel of the Lord, I ask that You cleanse me daily so that I will be a faithful servant in the house of the Lord.

Lord, as I stand as the messenger of the Lord of hosts, there is still joy in my heart as You send me out to the vineyards of the world. Because I know You go with me and I have nothing to fear. I continue to prepare my heart to seek the law of the Lord and to do it and teach it in the congregations. I am clothed with salvation and I rejoice in Your goodness.

I desire to be a faithful servant that will do all You have in your heart and mind for me to do. I will sow beside all waters, for I believe the fruit of the righteous is a tree of life, and the person that wins souls is wise. I thank You for the opportunity to be a minister according to Your heart, who will continue to feed Your people with knowledge and with understanding.

In Jesus name, amen.

Scripture References

Numbers 16:9	Isaiah 52:11
Jeremiah 1:7	1 Samuel 2:35
Isaiah 32:20	Jeremiah 3:15
Ezra 7:10	Jeremiah 20:9
Isaiah 26:3	2 Chronicles 6:41
Malachi 2:6,7	

Giving With Joy!

Lord, today I rise celebrating the life You have ordained for me! Thank You for each and every opportunity I have to labor in Your vineyard. I count it a joy to teach, preach, pray, and serve Your people. It is a privilege to share the Good News of the Gospel with those whom You allow to cross my path in the marketplace and in the house of the Lord.

I thank You for every child, teenager, young adult, adult, and senior who is a member of my congregation/ministry. I thank You for the privilege of leading many to a saving faith in Jesus Christ. I thank You for the different nations represented in both the congregation/ministry and community that my life has touched. I pray that the love of Christ in my heart has been made tangible with each encounter, for Your love is a love that can heal and help anyone You touch.

Lord, because You have given us all things richly to enjoy, I count it a privilege to be a generous giver of the gifts and graces that come from Your hand. Help me to remember the joy that comes from giving when I may not feel like it or when I think I need to be on the receiving end of things. Father, remind me daily that as You gave your greatest gift, I can always offer You as the living bread and water to every hungry and thirsty soul I encounter. In Your name I pray. Amen.

Scripture References

Jeremiah 1:7	Psalm 9:2
Daniel 12:3	Romans 5:5
Psalm 34:1	Psalm 126:5
Deuteronomy 12:18	1 Timothy 6:17

"I don't pray for success, I pray for faithfulness."

MOTHER TERESA

A Minister's Personal Prayer

Father, in the name of Jesus, I resolve to be as conscientious and responsible toward those who work with me in this congregation/ministry as I expect them to be toward me. I will not misuse the authority over them that You have placed in my hands, and I will not forget that I am responsible to a heavenly Shepherd, who makes no distinction between Shepherd and sheep.

As a minister I realize that my responsibility is to be just and fair toward those who labor with me in ministry. I purpose always to maintain the habit of prayer for them: to be alert and thankful as I pray for each person to find favor with You and with other people. Help me always to give honor where honor is due.

Give me Your discernment for those with whom I labor, that I might see their hidden potential and draw it out, helping them to become all that You created them to be. I value those who serve with me as persons called of You for their appointed tasks. I thank You for their abilities and talents, and I ask You to make me sensitive to their spiritual and emotional needs. Although I could be bold and order them to do what they ought to do, help me to always appeal to them on the basis of Your love.

Thank You for Your strength and ability, which enables me to do unto them as I would have them do unto me. Help me to follow Jesus as my example in all that I say and do. May we build your kingdom in joy, faith, and love to Your glory.

In Jesus name I pray, amen.

Scripture References

Ephesians 6:9 PHILLIPS

Colossians 4:1,2 PHILLIPS

Luke 2:52

Romans 13:7

Philemon 8-9 NIV

Matthew 7:12 NIV

1 Peter 2:21 NIV

"I feel no anxiety at the large armament designed against us. The remarkable interpositions of heaven in our favor cannot be too gratefully acknowledged. He who fed the Israelites in the wilderness, who clothes the lilies of the field and feeds the young ravens when they cry, will not forsake a people engaged in so right a cause, if we remember His loving kindness."

ABIGAIL ADAMS

A Minister's Prayer for Protection

Father, in the name of Jesus I pray for a hedge of protection to be placed round about my family and ministry. Thank You for being a wall of fire round about them and for assigning angels to watch over and protect them in all their ways of service and obedience.

In the name of Jesus I thank You, Father, that we dwell in the secret place of the Most High and abide under the shadow of the Almighty. I say of You, Lord, You are our refuge and fortress; in You will we trust. You cover my family and staff with Your feathers, and under Your wings shall we trust. We shall not be afraid of the terror by night or the arrow that flies by day. Only with our eyes will we behold and see the reward of the wicked.

Because we have made You, Lord, our refuge and fortress, no evil shall befall us, no accident will overtake us, and no plague or calamity shall come near us; for You give Your angels charge over us to keep us in all Your ways.

Father, because You have set Your love upon us, therefore You will deliver us. We shall call upon You, and You will answer. You will be with us in times of trouble, satisfy us with a long life, and show us Your salvation. Amen.

Scripture References

Ezekiel 22:30   Psalm 91:4,5 AMP

Zechariah 2:5   Psalm 91:8-11 AMP

Psalm 34:7

Psalm 91:1,2 AMP

Psalm 91:14-16 AMP

Luke 21:18

Section *IV*

PERSONAL PRAYERS FOR BUSINESS LEADERS

This book of the law shall not depart out of thy mouth; but thou shalt meditate therein day and night, that thou mayest observe to do according to all that is written therein: for then thou shalt make thy way prosperous, and then thou shalt have good success.

Joshua 1:8

Introduction

There is unlimited power in prayers that avail much.[1]

In the Scriptures, success is guaranteed to the person who gives Jesus preeminence in the world of business: "And he is the head of the body, the church: who is the beginning, the firstborn from the dead; that in all things he might have the preeminence. For it pleased the Father that in him should all fullness dwell."[2]

Before my husband retired he didn't leave the house until we gave thanks to God for the beginning of another day, acknowledged Jesus as Lord, and prayed for godly wisdom in every decision. We asked the Lord to make us a blessing to others and to give us favor and understanding in our respective places of business. "Honor God and give Him glory for your success: ...remember the Lord your God, for it is he who gives you the ability to produce wealth, and so confirms his covenant, which he swore to your forefathers, as it is today."[3]

Pray on every occasion, asking for godly wisdom without misgiving or reservation: "If any of you lacks wisdom, he should ask God, who gives generously to all without finding fault, and it will be given to him."[4]

---

[1] James 5:16 AMP

[2] Colossians 1:18,19

[3] Deuteronomy 8:18 NIV

[4] James 1:5 NIV

Prayer will bring personal changes in you and will produce conduct in you that will ensure your success in life. Jesus said of those who put their trust in Him, "I have come that they may have life, and have it to the full."[5] Financial success alone is not our standard, but Jesus himself is our Guide for victorious living at home and at work.

A scheduled time to pray scriptural prayers, read, and meditate on God's Word will reinforce your identification with Christ. In the marketplace your godly wisdom will calm troubled waters and your influence as a business leader will continue to increase. You will be known as a person of integrity who deals truly, speaks truly, and lives truly. Your life will be a testimony to the greatness and goodness of our Heavenly Father.

[5] John 10:10 NIV

"For in Jesus Christ, the light of the world, are hid all the treasures of wisdom and knowledge; redemption and glory."

WILLIAM PENN

FOUNDER OF PENNSYLVANIA

"There is a loftier ambition than merely to stand high in the world. It is to stoop down and lift mankind a little higher."

HENRY VAN DYKE (1852-1933)

AMERICAN AUTHOR, EDUCATOR, CLERGYMAN

Beginning the Business Day

Father, I come to You in the name of Jesus, asking You to give me the wisdom and knowledge to make decisions that are in keeping with Your Word and that will be beneficial to me and each one I come in contact with today.

This is the day which You have made, and I will be glad in it. I choose to submit to Your will today, that all my plans and purposes may be conducted in a manner that will bring honor and glory to You.

Thank You, Father, for Your direction and guidance; with it we can have good success. Thank You for the many blessings You have poured out upon us all.

Now to Him who is able to do immeasurably more than all we ask or imagine, according to His power that is at work within us, to Him be the glory in this company throughout all generations, forever and ever! In Jesus' name I pray. Amen.

Scripture References

Psalm 118:24	Lamentations 3:22,23
1 Samuel 15:22	Joshua 1:8
2 Timothy 1:12	Ephesians 3:14-17 NIV
Psalm 91:11,12 NIV	Ephesians 3:20 NIV

The Company

Father, I pray for _____ today. I thank You for this organization and for the opportunity to be a part of this business team. I am grateful for the chance to earn the income this firm provides for me and my family and for the blessing that it has been to me and all the employees.

Father, I thank You that _____ enjoys a good reputation. Thank You that our company prospers and makes a profit, and that You give us favor with our clients. I pray that You continue to provide wisdom and insight to those who occupy important decision-making positions. I thank You that _____ will continue to have a reputation of integrity in the community.

It is my prayer that _____ will continue to thrive and prosper. Thank You for increased sales and expanded markets.

Thank You, Father, for the creativity that is evident in the different areas of the company—new product ideas and new servicing concepts—innovations and techniques that keep this organization vibrant, alive, and thriving.

I ask You, Lord, to bless us and to cause us to be a blessing to the market we serve, as well as to all those whose lives are invested here on a daily basis.

In Jesus' name I pray, amen.

Scripture References

1 Timothy 2:1-3   Proverbs 3:21

3 John 2   Psalm 115:14

Joshua 1:8   Proverbs 8:12

Psalm 5:12   Malachi 3:12 AMP

Proverbs 2:7   Hebrews 6:14

"Almost every man who has by his life-work added to the sum of human achievement of which the race is proud, almost every such man had based his work largely upon the teachings of the Bible."

THEODORE ROOSEVELT

Company Executives

Father, in the name of Jesus, I thank You for the privilege of serving You as an employee here at _____. Thank You for sending Your Holy Spirit to teach me to pray for the good of the company, that Your name may be glorified.

I pray for those who are in positions of authority and leadership. I offer this prayer on behalf of the company executives, asking that You turn their hearts in the way that You would have them go.

I pray for the president and other officers, thanking You for their commitment and dedication to this organization. Thank You that they are upright and honest in all their business dealings. Thank You for providing them with new and creative ideas on how to better fulfill their duties and responsibilities and complete the tasks that You have entrusted to them.

Give our executives insight and understanding beyond their reason. Thank You for Your anointing upon them that goes far beyond their natural gifts and talents. Give them, I pray, clear and distinct direction so that they know what to do and how to do it. Grant them the vision to develop new ideas and concepts and the ability to implement them for the good of all concerned.

Help our leaders, Father, to be sensitive to the needs of every individual in this company. Give them the ability to balance the financial and human resources available to them.

Give them supernatural foresight and discernment
concerning personnel matters.

During these days of constant change, help those in
authority to maintain a positive attitude. Help them to count
it all joy when they fall into various trials, knowing that the
testing of their faith produces patience. Patience is a spiritual
force that will enable them to persevere.

Thank You, Father, that they receive all the pertinent
information necessary to make good and correct decisions.
Help me to be a blessing to them, to respect them and to
give honor where honor is due. May I always be an asset to
them and never a liability.

Thank You that when we pray in obedience to Your will
for those who occupy positions of authority or high responsibility, outwardly we will experience a quiet and undisturbed
life. and inwardly a peaceable one in all godliness, reverence,
and seriousness in every way.

Clothed in the armor of God, I stand against any pressure and anxiety that would cause our company executives to
make hasty or unwise decisions. Help them to discern
between good and bad choices and to make wise decisions—
decisions that will contribute to the growth of this company
and work for the benefit of every employee.

In Jesus' name I pray, amen.

Scripture References

2 Thessalonians 1:12

Proverbs 21:1

Psalm 25:21

Romans 12:17 NIV

Ephesians 1:9,17

Proverbs 3:5,6

Psalm 37:23 AMP

1 Timothy 2:1-3

Isaiah 33:6

James 1:2-4

Hebrews 10:35,36

2 Timothy 1:7

Ephesians 6:11-18

"Who can doubt that God created us to be happy, and thereto made us to love one another? It is plainly written as the Gospel. The heart is sometimes so embittered that nothing but Divine love can sweeten it, so enraged that devotion can only becalm it, and so broken down that it takes all the forces of heavenly hope to raise it. In short, the religion of Jesus Christ is the only sure and controlling power over sin."

FRANCIS MARION, "OLD SWAMP FOX"

MAJOR GENERAL, REVOLUTIONARY WAR

"An effective organization has a purpose that is shared by all its members and to which they will willingly commit their efforts. People working together can do almost anything."

J. L. HAYES

EDUCATOR AND FORMER PRESIDENT OF THE

AMERICAN MANAGEMENT ASSOCIATION

Dealing with Strife

Father, I come to You in the name that is above all other names—the name of Jesus. Your name is a strong tower that I can run into and be safe when I encounter strife on the job.

Lord, I admit that the accusations and unkind words spoken to me and about me really hurt. I desire to be accepted by my employer/co-workers/employees, but I long to obey You and follow Your commandments. I know that Jesus was tempted just as I am, but He didn't give in to sin or hate. Please give me Your mercy and grace to deal with this situation. I look to You for my comfort; You are a true Friend at all times.

Thank You, Lord, for never leaving me alone or rejecting me. I make a decision to forgive the people who have spoken unkind words about me. I ask You to work this forgiveness in my heart. I submit to You and reject the disappointment and anger that have attempted to consume me.

Specifically, right now I forgive _____.

I ask You to cause this situation to accommodate itself for good in my life and in the lives of others. To you, O Lord, I lift up my soul; in You I trust, O my God. Do not let me be put to shame, nor let my enemies triumph over me. I pray that You will have mercy upon them.

Because I love You, O Lord, You will rescue me; You will protect me because I acknowledge Your name. I will call upon You, and You will deliver me; You will be with me in trouble; You will deliver me and honor me.

Father, I will resist the temptation to strike back in anger. I purpose to love _____ with the love of Jesus in me. Mercy and truth are written upon the tablets of my heart; therefore, You will cause me to find favor and understanding with my employer, co-workers, and employees. Keep me from self-righteousness so that I may walk in Your righteousness.

Thank You for giving me friends who will stand by me and teach me how to guard my heart with all diligence.

I declare that in the midst of all these things I am more than a conqueror through Jesus, who loves me. I can use the witty inventions You have provided me, and I will be confident in Your wisdom when working. I am of good courage and pray that freedom of utterance be given to me as I do my job.

In Jesus' name I pray, amen.

Scripture References

Philippians 2:9	Proverbs 3:3,4
Psalm 25:1,2 NIV	Proverbs 18:10
Proverbs 4:23	Hebrews 4:15
Romans 8:37	Proverbs 17:17
Proverbs 8:12	Hebrews 13:5
Psalm 31:24	Proverbs 16:4 AMP
Ephesians 6:19	Psalm 91:14,15 NIV

Employees

Father, in the name of Jesus I desire that the work of our hands, our labor in the department/office here at
_____ be productive for Your glory and for the good and profit of all. You have given us everything we need to live a full and useful life.

We are individuals who are [mutually dependent on one another], having gifts that differ according to the grace given us. We, who with unveiled faces all reflect Your glory, are being transformed into Your likeness with ever-increasing glory, which comes from You.

Father, I realize that You know what we have need of before we ask, and that we are not all growing in the same manner or on the same time schedule, but we are growing in the grace and knowledge of our Lord and Savior, Jesus Christ.

We give each other space to grow, for we are becoming a patient people, bearing with one another. We acknowledge that we do not have dominion [over] each other, and we refuse to lord it over one another's faith, but we are fellow laborers to promote one another's joy, because it is by faith that we stand strong.

In Jesus' name I pray, amen.

Scripture References

2 Peter 1:3,4

2 Peter 3:18

Romans 12:5,6 AMP

2 Corinthians 1:24 AMP

2 Corinthians 3:18 NIV

Ephesians 4:2 AMP

Matthew 6:32

"Being in power is like being a lady.
If you have to tell people you are,
you aren't."

MARGARET THATCHER

PRIME MINISTER OF GREAT BRITAIN
(1979-1990)

An Employer's Personal Prayer

Father, in the name of Jesus I resolve to be as conscientious and responsible toward those who work for me as I expect them to be toward me. I will not misuse the power over others that has been placed in my hands, and I will not forget that I am responsible myself to a heavenly Supervisor who makes no distinction between employer and employee.

As an employer I realize that my responsibility is to be just and fair toward those I employ. I purpose always to maintain the habit of prayer for them: to be alert and thankful as I pray for each person to find favor with You and with other people. Help me always to give honor where honor is due.

Give me Your discernment for those with whom I labor, that I might see their hidden potential and draw it out, helping them to become all that You created them to be.

I value my employees as persons called of You for their appointed tasks. I thank You for their abilities and talents, and I ask You to make me sensitive to their spiritual and emotional needs. Although I could be bold and order my associates to do what they ought to do, help me to appeal to them always on the basis of Your love.

Thank You for Your power and ability, which enable me to do unto them as I would have them do unto me. Help me to follow Jesus as my example in all that I say and do. In His name I pray, amen.

Scripture References

Ephesians 6:9 PHILLIPS

Colossians 4:1,2 PHILLIPS

Luke 2:52

Romans 13:7

Philemon 8,9 NIV

Matthew 7:12 NIV

1 Peter 2:21 NIV

"Leadership is the capacity to translate vision into reality."

WARREN G. BENNIS

AUTHOR, SCHOLAR ON LEADERSHIP

PRAYERS THAT AVAIL MUCH

FOR LEADERS

Practicing Good Communication in Business

Father, I will show appreciation for a job well done. My words of appreciation shall be honest and sincere. I am not merely concerned with my own interests but also for the interests of others. I show honor where honor is due, acknowledge people by name with respect, and make the other person feel important with my communication.

Give me a listening ear so I will understand what they are saying. I nourish myself on the truths of the faith and of the good instruction which I closely follow. I resist the temptation to get caught up with trifling (ill-informed, unedifying, stupid controversy) over ignorant questionings, for I know that they foster strife and breed quarrels.

Bring to the light any prejudices and wrong attitudes that I may have. Expose insecurities that push me into being self-defensive and accusing the other person of being wrong. When anything is exposed and reproved by the light, it is made visible and clear; and where everything is visible and clear, there is light. Your light dispels the darkness, and I have no need for self-aggrandizement and self-promotion.

Teach me to guard my heart with all diligence, for out of it flow the very issues of life. Thank You for giving me discernment as I listen to the ideas and opinions of others, especially when they are different than mine.

The power of life and death are in the tongue, and You said that I would eat the fruit of it. A word out of my mouth may seem of no account, but it can accomplish nearly anything—or destroy anything!

Father, forgive me for criticizing and judging others harshly. Forgive me for those times when I have knowingly or unknowingly twisted the truth to make myself sound wise; the times I have tried to look better than others; the times my words have contributed to things falling apart. I receive and thank You for forgiveness, and now I forgive myself; You are cleansing me from all unrighteousness.

Father, I ask for wisdom that is from above and submit to the wisdom that begins with a holy life and is characterized by getting along with others. Use me as Your instrument in developing a God-fearing, healthy organization. I will enjoy its results only if I do the hard work of getting along with others, treating them with dignity and honor.

My tongue is as choice silver, and my lips feed and guide many. I open my mouth in skillful and godly wisdom to give counsel and instructions. Lord, You are my God and I love You with all my heart, soul, and mind. And I will love others as well as I love myself.

In the name of Jesus I pray, amen.

Scripture References

1 Timothy 2:23	1 John 3:1
Ephesians 4:29 NIV	Matthew 6:6

Psalm 45:1 AMP

Proverbs 3:3 AMP

Proverbs 8:6-8 AMP

Proverbs 10:20,21 AMP

Proverbs 31:26 AMP

Romans 8:31-39 NIV

Hebrews 2:11 NIV

John 15:15 NIV

John 14:26

Revelation 12:11

Hebrews 11:6 AMP

Ephesians 5:13 AMP

Proverbs 4:23

Ephesians 4:15

Proverbs 18:21

James 3:5,6 THE MESSAGE

James 3:9-16 THE MESSAGE

James 3:17

James 3:17,18 THE MESSAGE

"I always told God: I'm gwine to hole stiddy on to You, and You got to see me trou…Jes so long as He wants to use me, He'll tak ker of me."

HARRIET TUBMAN (1821-1913)

FORMER SLAVE, RISKED HER LIFE TO ESTABLISH THE UNDERGROUND RAILROAD

Planning for Successful Travel

Today, I confess God's Word over our travel plans. As my co-workers and I prepare to travel, I rejoice in the promises that God's Word holds for protection and safety of the righteous. Father, You alone make us live in safety. I trust in You and dwell in Your protection. Believing in the written Word of God, I speak peace, safety, and success over the travel plans for my business associates, in Jesus' name.

As a child of God, our path of travel is preserved, and angels keep charge over us. We will proceed with our travel plans without fear of accidents, problems, or any type of frustrations. Lord, thank You for delivering us from every type of evil and preserving us for Your kingdom. I stand confident that our travel plans will not be disrupted or confused.

Thank You, Father, that in every situation You are there to protect us. No matter in what means of transportation we choose to travel, You have redeemed us and will protect us. The earth and all things on it are under Your command. You are my Heavenly Father. Through my faith in You, I have the power to tread over the power of the enemy, and no food or water will harm us when we arrive at our destination.

Father, I give You the glory in this situation. Thank You that as I keep Your ways before me, we will be safe. Your mercy is upon me and my associates, and our travels will be safe. Thank You, Father, for Your guidance and safety—You are worthy of all praise! Amen.

Scripture References

Isaiah 55:11

Jeremiah 1:12

Psalm 4:8

Psalm 91:1

Proverbs 18:10

Proverbs 29:25

Mark 11:23,24

Proverbs 2:8

Psalm 91:11,12

2 Timothy 4:18

Philippians 4:7

2 Timothy 1:7

Isaiah 43:1-3

2 Timothy 4:18

Hosea 2:18

Luke 10:19

Psalm 91:13

Luke 21:18

Mark 16:18

Matthew 18:18

John 14:13

Daniel 9:18

Luke 1:50

"What other nation is so great to have their gods near them the way the Lord our God is near us whenever we pray to him?"

DEUTERONOMY 4:7

Making a Difficult Decision

Father, I bring this decision before You. It is a difficult one for me to make in the natural, but I know that with You it can be an easy one.

I ask You, Lord, to help me see both sides of this issue and to consider all the facts involved in it. Help me to properly evaluate both the positive and negative attributes of this situation. I ask You to surround me with wise counsel. Help me to ask for help or to be open for insight from mature sources.

Lord, I recognize that an important part of being an excellent manager is decisiveness. In processing the information and considering the possible repercussions or benefits of this decision, help me to avoid the paralysis of analysis. Help me to get the information I need and to evaluate it carefully and wisely.

Help me, Father, to hear Your voice, and so to make the right and correct decision in this case. Keep me from acting in haste but also from delaying too long to reach a decision.

Father, help me not to be influenced by my own personal wants or desires concerning this matter under consideration. Instead, help me to perceive and choose what is best for my department or company, regardless of how I may feel about it personally. Help me to undertake and carry out this decision-making process accurately and objectively.

Thank You for Your guidance and direction in this situation.

In Jesus' name I pray, amen.

Scripture References

Isaiah 11:2 AMP	John 10:27
Colossians 4:1 NIV	Philippians 2:3 NIV
Proverbs 28:1	Judges 6:12

Undertaking a New Initiative

Lord, I lift up to You this new initiative which we are considering. I feel that it is one we should be a part of, something we should do, but I seek Your wisdom concerning it.

If it is of You, Father, then I thank You for Your counsel and assistance concerning it. Give us understanding and discernment in the preparation stages as we gather the information we need to devise a course of action and to plan the budget. Help us to accumulate the facts and figures we need to carry out this plan in accordance with Your will and purpose.

Thank You, Lord, for Your insight and wisdom. I ask You to give each of us guidance and direction by Your Holy Spirit so we will know how to assimilate the information we gather and use it to maximum advantage. Reveal to us any hidden costs or expenses so that we can take them into account in preparing an accurate budget and detailed forecast of both time and money.

Give all of us involved in this project the ability to concentrate our attention and focus our efforts so that we can successfully complete this undertaking and thereby bring honor and glory to You.

In Jesus' name I pray, amen.

Scripture References

Proverbs 8:12 AMP

Isaiah 11:2 NIV

Jeremiah 29:11-13

Jeremiah 33:3 NIV

Ephesians 1:8,9,17 AMP

Luke 12:2 NIV

Romans 12:2 NIV

"The best way to cheer yourself up is to cheer everybody else up."

MARK TWAIN

Encouraging Employees

Father, I pray for every employee of this organization. I ask that You give me wisdom in my interaction with them. Help me to recognize and develop their individual strengths. I purpose to provide them with the necessary tools and resources to get their jobs done. Make me sensitive to their needs, both personal and professional.

Lord, grant me the wisdom to balance the tangible, strategic, and tactical aspects of every decision with the intangible, sensitive, and human aspects involved. Cause me to see my employees as people and not merely as workers, and show me how to bring out the best in each of them.

Help me, Father, to speak truly, live truly, and deal truly. Give me the ability to communicate to them clearly what I expect from them. I pray that I will deal fairly and honestly with them, to praise them when they do well and to correct them with a gentle spirit when they make errors.

May I always focus on the performance and never the performers, so that even after correction they still feel encouraged and excited about their work with a full understanding of what needs to be done to change or correct the specific action under review. I purpose to always give honor and praise where honor and praise are appropriate.

I pray for their families, Lord. Bless them financially and physically. Grant them health and wholeness and provide for their needs abundantly.

Help them, Lord, to realize that strife, gossip, and back-biting are destructive forces which will, in the end, not only negatively affect the corporation but, more seriously, destroy them spiritually.

Raise up among their ranks Joshuas and Calebs and make them evident to me. Give me insight on who to promote and where to place them for maximum advantage. I thank You, Father, for sending us good people—qualified and dedicated men and women to do the jobs that need to be done. I thank You that they are anointed of You. You have said that those You call, You also anoint, and that those You anoint, You also equip. Thank You for Your anointing to get the job done above and beyond our own strengths, abilities, gifts, and talents.

In Jesus' name I pray, amen.

Scripture References

2 Chronicles 35:2 AMP

Psalm 45:1 NIV

1 Timothy 5:21 NIV

James 3:17 AMP

Hebrews 13:21 AMP

Matthew 25:21

1 Peter 2:14 AMP

Proverbs 29:19 AMP

3 John 2 AMP

2 Corinthians 7:4

Luke 6:38 NIV

James 3:2 AMP

2 Corinthians 1:21 AMP

1 John 2:27 AMP

Matthew 25:23 NIV

Hiring a New Employee

Father, I come to You concerning the position that is available in our company. I believe that for every individual You created You have a perfect will, plan, and purpose.

Lord, I ask You to send the right person for this job, a person who is Your perfect choice to fill the vacant position in our midst at this time in their life. If Your chosen individual is already working in this organization, thank You for revealing to us who they are. If that perfect someone is not currently employed by our company, then I ask You to draw that individual here.

Father, in 2 Chronicles 22:15 You told Solomon that You would send him workmen who were talented and cunning for every manner of work. We seek someone who has the right gifts and talents for this job, someone with the right character and personality, the right personal attributes. We seek someone who has a spirit and attitude that are pleasing to You; someone whose character, integrity, and morality are above reproach; someone who will be an outstanding employee and an excellent co-worker; someone who is willing to accept responsibility and take on new challenges; someone who will be a great leader; someone who will rise to the occasion; someone who is committed and faithful to give their best to whatever they do.

Thank You for an individual who will be supportive of those in positions of leadership and will pray for and cooperate with them.

Lord, we want people who are interested in building Your kingdom, who know how to submit to authority while maintaining their own independence, for we are mutually dependent on one another. We ask for self-starters and self-motivators.

Father, we are looking for a person of humility, who will stand up for what is right. Send us a thinker. Send us someone who is teachable, eager to learn and to take up new duties and responsibilities.

I thank You, Lord, that in the interview process You will reveal to us the precise individual for the position that is open.

Father, not our will, but Yours be done. I thank You for sending just the perfect individual, called and anointed of You, to fill this position.

In Jesus' name I pray, amen.

Scripture References

Jeremiah 29:11	Proverbs 21:5
Romans 8:28	Luke 9:62
Daniel 1:17	1 Timothy 2:1-3
Daniel 9:22	Ephesians 5:21,22
Psalm 25:21	1 Peter 3:8
Proverbs 12:3	1 John 2:27
Proverbs 19:1	

Serving Consumers

Father, I thank You for those that do business with us because without them we could not stay in business.

Thank You, Lord, for all those who buy our products or use our services. Help us to be more sensitive to their needs and more responsive to their wants and desires. Help us to serve them better, because it is in serving our consumers better that our company grows and prospers.

Help us to be on the lookout for ways to provide better products/services. Show us how we can be more sensitive to the needs of our clients.

Help us, Lord, always to have a hearing ear to what our consumers have to say concerning our products/services. Help us to respond quickly and effectively to those areas they call to our attention.

Father, I pray that our relationships will be pleasant and memorable, that we will bring joy and peace to the hearts of all we serve. Help us always to remember that in helping to fulfill their needs, desires, and wants, we are creating a strong, long-lasting relationship between us and them that will profit both of us and be a blessing to many others.

In Jesus' name I pray, amen.

Scripture References

Galatians 5:13

Psalm 115:14

Philippians 2:7

Proverbs 8:12

Proverbs 2:2

Romans 15:13

Section V

THE SEVEN MOUNTAINS PRAYER STRATEGY

It shall come to pass in the latter days
that the mountain of the Lord's house shall
be [firmly] established as the highest of the
mountains and shall be exalted above the
hills, and all nations shall flow to it.

Isaiah 2:2

Introduction

The prayers in this section are based on *The Seven Mountain Prophecy* by Johnny Enlow, senior pastor of Daystar International Christian Fellowship in Atlanta, Georgia. He ministers in Latin American countries where he has favor with high-level spiritual, economic, and political leaders—including several heads of state.

Pastor Enlow gives strategies for reclaiming our society for the kingdom of God. His message of hope is inspiring as he shares his God-given revelation of a modern-day Elijah revolution which will impact the seven culture-shaping areas of influence over society, which includes media, government, education, economy, family, arts and entertainment, and religion.

I recommend that you read and learn from this intensive, detailed study of each "mountain" of influence and how they can be transformed. The church is called to get involved in God's plan for mankind.

The prayer movements of the past few decades prepared the way for this present time, but we must not relax our stand. Having done all to stand, we stand. The Holy Spirit is helping us as we continue pressing in to see the will of God done on earth even as it is in heaven.

This is not a one-person agenda. According to Ephesians 2, God raised us up together with Him and made us sit down together [giving us joint seating with Him] in the heavenly sphere [by virtue of our being] in Christ Jesus (the Messiah, the Anointed One). Together we make up the one new man created in Christ Jesus our Lord. United in prayer we will proclaim and decree that His will shall be done on earth even as it is in heaven. The seven mountains will be restored and transformed according to godly principles if we will learn to get along with each other, learn to be considerate of one another, and cultivate a life in common.[1]

Ask the Holy Spirit to reveal to you your place of prayer as the church climbs these mountains for kingdom purposes, that the whole earth might be filled with the glory of God. You are not called to take every level of all the mountains alone. It will take the united body of Christ working together. As an example, the media outlets include television and radio stations and networks (local, national, and international), websites, newspapers, books, and magazines. He may assign you to pray for a specific outlet in your city or certain newscasters by name.

The following prayers are beginning prayers. As you continue to pray the Holy Spirit will usher you into higher levels of spiritual worship and warfare.

---

[1]   1 Corinthians 1:10 The Message

"The foundations of our society and our government rest so much on the teachings of the Bible that it would be difficult to support them if faith in these teachings would cease to be practically universal in our country."

CALVIN COOLIDGE

"There is no leveler like Christianity, but it levels by lifting all who receive it to the lofty table-land of a true character and of undying hope both for this world and the next."

JONATHAN EDWARDS

Introductory Prayer for the Seven Mountains of Society

Father, I come to You in the name of Jesus and thank You for the Holy Spirit, who helps me pray when I don't know how. In times past You instructed Daniel to shut up the words and seal the Book until the time of the end. The Book is now opened and the knowledge of Your purposes is being revealed by Your prophets, who are increased and have become great.

Praise the name of Jesus, who is the Lion of the tribe of Judah, the Root (Source) of David, who has won (overcome and conquered)! I worship You. You have opened the scroll and even now You are breaking its seven seals! You are the Lamb standing, as though it had been slain, with seven horns and with seven eyes, which are the seven Spirits of God [the sevenfold Holy Spirit], who have been sent [on duty far and wide] into all the earth.

Open my eyes that I might behold You as You take the scroll from the right hand of Him who sits on the throne. I see the four living creatures and the twenty-four elders [of the heavenly Sanhedrin] prostrating themselves before the Lamb. Each is holding a harp (lute or guitar), and they have golden bowls full of incense (fragrant spices and gums for burning), which are the prayers of God's people (the saints).

Oh, my Father, my Lord, even now I join them in the new song, saying, "Jesus, You are worthy to take the scroll and to break the seals that are on it, for You were slain (sacrificed), and with Your blood. You purchased men unto God from every tribe and language and people and nation. And You have made us a kingdom (royal race) of priests to our God, and we shall reign [as kings] over the earth!"

Father, even now I hear the voices of many angels on every side of the throne and of the living creatures and the elders [of the heavenly Sanhedrin], and they number ten thousand times ten thousand and thousands of thousands. We join them saying in a loud voice, "Deserving is the Lamb, who was sacrificed, to receive all the power and riches and wisdom and might and honor and majesty (glory, splendor) and blessing!"

Amen! Amen! And amen!

Scripture References

Daniel 12:4   Revelation 5

Foundation Prayer for Intercession

Father, we cry out for understanding, and may this become our reality as we begin this prayer journey preparing the way of the Lord. Thank You for the Spirit, who testifies together with our own spirit, [assuring us] that we are children of God. And if we are [His] children, then we are [His] heirs also: heirs of God and fellow heirs with Christ [sharing His inheritance with Him]; only we must share His suffering if we are to share His glory.

[But what of that?] For I consider that the sufferings of this present time (this present life) are not worth being compared with the glory that is about to be revealed to us and in us and for us and conferred on us!

For [even the whole] creation (all nature) waits expectantly and longs earnestly for God's sons to be made known [waits for the revealing, the disclosing of their sonship]. For the creation (nature) was subjected to frailty (to futility, condemned to frustration), not because of some intentional fault on its part, but by the will of Him who so subjected it—[yet] with the hope that nature (creation) itself will be set free from its bondage to decay and corruption [and gain an entrance] into the glorious freedom of God's children. We know that the whole creation [of irrational creatures] has been moaning together in the pains of labor until now.

And not only the creation, but we ourselves too, who have and enjoy the firstfruits of the [Holy] Spirit [a foretaste

of the blissful things to come] groan inwardly as we wait for
the redemption of our bodies [from sensuality and the grave,
which will reveal] our adoption (our manifestation as God's
sons). For in [this] hope we were saved. But hope [the object
of] which is seen is not hope. For how can one hope for
what he already sees? But if we hope for what is still unseen
by us, we wait for it with patience and composure.

So too the [Holy] Spirit comes to our aid and bears us up
in our weakness; for we do not know what prayer to offer nor
how to offer it worthily as we ought, but the Spirit himself
goes to meet our supplication and pleads in our behalf with
unspeakable yearnings and groanings too deep for utterance.
And He who searches the hearts of men knows what is in the
mind of the [Holy] Spirit [what His intent is], because the
Spirit intercedes and pleads [before God] in behalf of the
saints according to and in harmony with God's will.

We are assured and know that [God being a partner in
our labor] all things work together and are [fitting into a
plan] for good to and for those who love God and are called
according to [His] design and purpose.

Thank You for helping us pray effectively in the secret
place. We decree that You shall reward us openly, and our
nation shall experience a spiritual revolution for good and not
for evil.

Scripture References

Romans 8:16-28   Matthew 6:4

"And better had they ne'er been born,
Who read to doubt, or read to scorn."

SIR WALTER SCOTT

FROM CHAPTER XII OF *THE MONASTERY*

The Media

Father, open the eyes of our understanding that we might see and understand the power You have invested in Your church. You seated us together in heavenly places in Christ Jesus far above all principality, and power, and might, and dominion, and every name that is named, not only in this world, but also in that which is to come. We ask Your forgiveness for rejecting that which you ordained to be an evangelistic tool. We allowed the enemy to take control of the media, filling the newspapers and airwaves with bad news, fear-filled words, doubt, and unbelief; for this we repent.

Thank You for calling and equipping Your people to work in this industry, and thank You for human resource departments that recognize their credentials when they are applying for employment. We declare that they are as wise as serpents and harmless as doves. You cause them to find favor and good understanding with the managers and controllers of newspapers, magazines, and television and radio outlets.

We pray for Your will to be done in the media even as it is in heaven and ask that the morning news programs give hope to the hearers. Your plans for us are for welfare and not for evil, to give us a future and a hope.

We worship the King of kings and the Lord of lords, and pronounce judgment upon the powers of darkness that have ruled this mountain. The ruler (evil genius, prince) of this world [Satan] is judged and condemned, and sentence already is passed upon him. Having on the full armor of God, we enforce the triumphant victory of Jesus Christ won at Calvary and proclaim that where sin abounds grace does much more abound.

In His mighty name we shout, "Light be!" on this mountain. Darkness cannot overcome the light! We declare and decree that this mountain is filled with God-fearing men and women, the new evangelists who will speak truly, deal truly, and live truly. We say that God shall be properly centered so the compass for a proper worldview is carried throughout the airwaves and newspapers, charging the atmosphere with truth.

We decree that the airwaves will be filled with whatever things are true, whatever things are noble, whatever things are just, whatever things are pure, whatever things are lovely, whatever things are of good report; if there is any virtue and if there is anything praiseworthy it shall be reported, in the name of Jesus. Amen.

Scripture References

Ephesians 2:6

Ephesians 1:21

Ephesians 4:12

Matthew 10:16

Jeremiah 29:11

John 13:11

John 1:5

Ephesians 4:15

Philippians 4:8

"If America is to survive we must elect more God-centered men and women to public office."

BILLY GRAHAM

"I am much afraid that schools will prove to be the great gates of hell unless they diligently labor in explaining the Holy Scriptures, engraving them in the hearts of youth. I advise no one to place his child where the Scriptures do not reign paramount."

MARTIN LUTHER

The Government

Lord, give us leaders who know how to cultivate the ground of this nation; leaders who want to prepare our nation for the advancement of the kingdom of God and not their own name; men and women who do not desire to be famous but faithful, pursuing righteousness and justice with boldness and uncompromising adherence to Your Word; leaders who will esteem You with humble and contrite spirits; those who tremble at Your Word.

When they take elected offices, these men and women will rise above double mindedness and walk in God's calling upon their lives. They will be balanced officials, who aren't wrapped up in calculating and pursuing their own agendas, nor too tolerant, embracing strange fire upon the altars of this nation, accepting everything while lacking convictions to Your truths. These leaders will keep their spirits quiet and in tune with You—having self-control of their passions which wield great power and strength—in times of great difficulty and great expectations.

May all our governmental authorities quickly obey Your voice of instruction and leave fleshly wisdom and familiar counselors outside the camp. Give them Your anointing to increase their spiritual influence in the work environment. May all political appointees ascend Capitol Hill and assume their offices with clean hands and pure hearts. Give them Your light and Your truth to lead us to the rock that is higher than us.

May we forgive those who have transgressed and stirred up and contaminated waters that were once clean and pure and flowed from Your throne into our land, those who have taken the best for themselves and trampled and despised the blessings You gave to us when You ordained our great nation. May we awaken and shake ourselves from the dust of their pollutants and sit once again in a dignified place. When our ways please You, You will fight for us, and even our enemies must live at peace with us.

Thank You, Lord, for leaders who carry Your plumb line in their pockets so our foundations will be repaired and fortified, and our political offices will comprise the watchmen of the Lord.

Father, raise up Your righteous ones who are under Your authority before they become a governing authority while in office. We ask you to keep them clear-minded, looking forward to the days of Your visitation. Encourage Your people that godly leaders are on the way as we resolutely separate the precious from the vile and return to You.

Adapted from *Government Leaders*
Copyright © 2007 Lynn K. Thomas
President/Co-founder Intercessors
International, Inc. Used by permission.

Scripture References

Genesis 2:5	Psalm 101:6
Isaiah 66:2	James 1:5-8

Psalm 12:8

Psalm 24:3,4

Ezekiel 34:18,19

Proverbs 16:7

Amos 7: 7-9

Isaiah 64:1-5

Jeremiah 15:19

Isaiah 30:15

Psalm 61:2

Isaiah 62:1

Deuteronomy 3:2

1 Peter 4:7

Isaiah 42:16

Education

Father we come to You in the precious and holy name of Jesus, acknowledging that You are our great and wise Teacher. We declare that You are all powerful, all knowing, and You are the Creator of all things that ever were or are to come. With the fruit of our lips we declare that to You and You alone be all glory, honor, dominion, and power forever and ever.

We declare that all wisdom and truth come from You and You alone. We acknowledge that just as You are the God of all wisdom, it is Your desire to bless us with wisdom in all things. Your Word says that if any of us lack wisdom, let us ask of God, that giveth to all [men] liberally, and upbraideth not; and it shall be given us.

Lord, our founding fathers desired to develop an educational system that would glorify You through our children's early years and ultimately train them with Your wisdom to go into the marketplace and take dominion over everything that exalts itself against Your truth and the knowledge of You.

Lord, we repent for having moved away from Your founding principles of our educational system. We repent for having built a system filled with educational policies and standards that have caused our students to turn their hearts from You. We ask that You forgive us for allowing the curriculum of evolution that denies Your existence to be taught in our schools. Forgive us for accepting the lies of the enemy in exchange for the truth, which is Your Word.

Take the scales off of the eyes of the educational policy makers, the educational leaders, the teachers, and the students so they may see You are the Living God and the Creator of all things. Lord, touch the hearts of the educators so they may turn their faces toward You and walk uprightly in Your ways.

Restore the ancient paths of educational principles that our father of education Horace Mann built through the inspiration of Your Holy Spirit, Lord. His ultimate vision for education was that everything we learned be used as a vehicle to glorify You while advancing the kingdom for Your name's sake. Oh, that You would fill our educational leaders, teachers, and policy makers with the desire to restore the ancient education foundations!

We ask You to place godly leaders in places of educational authority, that Your name be glorified as they watch over our educational system in all truth and righteousness. We ask You to pour out Your spirit upon our educational leaders and give them a fresh anointing to speak life and restoration to the teachers, parents, and students.

O Heavenly Father, we ask You to touch our teachers and fill their hearts with Your love and compassion for their students. Fill them with the love and compassion You have for children. You said in Your Word to suffer little children and forbid them not to come to You, for such is the kingdom of heaven. We especially ask You to fill them with Your abundant mercy and compassion for those who struggle to retain knowledge and those who express their anger and hurt though violence and aggression.

Father, help teachers to realize they have the awesome responsibility of sowing seeds of knowledge and hope as they shape our future. Oh, what an awesome honor You have bestowed on our educators! Heavenly Father, we ask You to stir up the gift of teaching in those who have lost their passion for it.

Father, we pray for the children who are precious in Your sight. Your Word says that all our children shall be taught of the Lord; and great shall be the peace of our children. Lord, we pray for the children to be filled with peace, wisdom, knowledge, and hearts that seek Your face. We pray You will place a hedge of protection around Your precious ones. Train them to turn a deaf ear to the lie of evolution. Send godly educators to our schools to watch over them in prayer.

In this day we pray You would touch this generation and raise up a new generation that would seek Your face, o God of Jacob. Heavenly Father, these things we ask in Your name. We thank You that Your Word never returns void, and You and You alone are able to do exceeding abundantly, far above all we could ask or think through the working of Your mighty power. Amen and amen!

By Monica Batiste
Educator
Written for *Prayers That Avail Much*® *for Leaders*

Scripture References

Jude 1:25

Luke 18:16

James 1:5

Isaiah 54:3

"Commerce alone will not make a nation great and happy like England. England has become great by the knowledge of the true God through Jesus Christ."

QUEEN ELIZABETH I OF ENGLAND

"It was wonderful to see the change soon made in the manners of our inhabitants. From being thoughtless or indifferent about religion, it seemed as if all the world were growing religious, so that one could not walk thro' the town in an evening without hearing psalms sung in different families of every street."

BENJAMIN FRANKLIN

(ON GEORGE WHITFIELD'S PREACHING)

The Economy

Our Father, which art in heaven, hallowed be Thy name. Thy kingdom come, Thy will be done on earth as it is in heaven.

In Jesus' name we are calling for powerful leaders who will speak truly, live truly, and deal truly; who will walk in integrity in trade and commerce. They will lean not unto their own understanding but in all their ways acknowledge You, and You shall direct their paths. We decree that they understand and promote the proper flow and balance of the production of resources, the distribution of resources, and the consumption of resources. We come before You, Father, to stand in the gap and build up the hedge for the prevention of the breakdown and corruption between production and distribution of wealth.

We ask for unpresumptuous economic leaders who trust in the Living God, who ask for and receive wisdom and understanding. Father, thank You for appointing and anointing leaders who live under the banner of the Lord's provision—those who put their faith in Jehovah-Jireh—the One who delights in providing for all His children.

Father, we thank You for financial leaders who declare the lordship of Jesus, who is seated at Your right hand in heaven, far above any other king or ruler or dictator or leader, including the principality of mammon, greed, and poverty.

Clothed in Your armor we withstand the deception of the god of this world—the antichrist.

We pray that these leaders will have ears to hear the [Holy] Spirit and will receive the gifts and utterances of the prophets with great appreciation. They will seek out prophetic revelations and inspired instruction or exhortation or warning. They will test and prove all things [until they can recognize] what is good, and to that they will hold fast. Greed shall be far from them because they abstain from evil. The power they exercise will be for the good of the people rather than for their own self-aggrandizement. We decree that they will not lord it over others but will serve people and be helpers of their joy in the name of the Lord Jesus.

Today we take this mountain of economy for the kingdom of God and will do according to all that He has commanded us. These leaders will be governed by the law of love, giving tithes and offerings. They shall feed the hungry and give them something to drink, they will welcome strangers, shelter and clothe them, provide help for the sick and infirmed, and minister truth to those in prison.

Jesus has come that we might have life and have it more abundantly, to the full till it overflows. Thank You, Father, that as You bless us and we bless others, they will praise You and give You thanks and bless others. Thus, the circle of Your love and blessing will go on and on into eternity.

You are Jehovah-Jireh, the One who sees our needs and provides for them. Hallowed be Thy name!

Scripture References

Matthew 6:9,10

Ephesians 4:15

Proverbs 3:5,6

Ezekiel 22:30

James 1:5

John 21:15

1 Corinthians 14:22

2 Corinthians 1:24

Matthew 25:35

John 10:10

Genesis 22:14

Religion

Father, by the example of sending Your Son to purchase us through His sacrificial death, You have shown us the meaning of true love. Your Word has taught us that we are called to love one another. In this way the world will know we have passed from death to life. The church is called to walk in love because You are love.

We pray the spiritual leaders will come alive to a fresh passion and fire for You. We pray the places where the church gathers to worship will explode into houses of glory. We pray we will see an increase of miracles, signs, and wonders that will make the Gospel come alive to those outside of the body of Christ at this time.

We recognize that there is a need for the breath of God to blow with increasing intensity across this nation and our world. Let the church hear Your invitation again to draw near to You and know that You will draw near to us. Teach us to return to times of waiting on You, just soaking in Your presence and learning to center our hearts in Yours. Open our ears to hear You speak Your will, plan, and purpose for the church in this hour.

We repent for all the ways we have allowed idolatry and antichrist spirits to infiltrate our lives and our worship. You are holy, and in many ways we have moved away from a walk of purity and holiness before You. Our hearts are hungry for the fullness of your presence in our midst. Our hearts are hungry for a passionate praise and worship that consumes our being. Cleanse us from dead works and old wineskins. Break and destroy every wall of tradition that has trapped us in lifeless worship and empty rituals. We pray the church will reflect a true picture of the kingdom of God as we gather together to worship from every tribe and nation. Create in us a clean heart and renew a right spirit within us.

Father, we pray those called to serve in the five-fold ministry offices would experience fresh zeal. Call them to the secret place with You so they can encounter Your glory again and receive new vision for Your church. Let them see Christ and Him crucified, and nothing but Jesus revealed. May a new generation of apostles, prophets, evangelists, pastors, and teachers arise, bound together in the depths of Your love. Let them speak in Your authority, walk with Your humility, and learn to yield to the plans You have for each of them for the furtherance of Your kingdom.

In the name of Jesus we believe the church of Jesus Christ is learning to walk in love and the power of the Holy Spirit. We are not a church that will continue to be divided by denominations or points of doctrine, but we are a church saturated by prayer and passionate worship of You, our God and King. We pray to become a church that, by our lives, will witness to a world in need of the love of Jesus. We pray to become a church that begins today to explode in waves of revival that will bring life to lifeless congregations and ignite the youngest believers to do exploits to the glory of God.

We pray in the name of Jesus that those persons crying out to know truth would encounter the living Lord through dynamic congregations. We pray for them to see the demonstration and power of the Holy Spirit that transforms lives. We pray for those that have explored other avenues of spirituality to encounter reality in Jesus Christ. May the church become an embodiment of the prayers prayed by Jesus.

We thank You for a move of God in the house of God. We pray always for the peace of Jerusalem. In the name of Jesus we pray. Amen.

Scripture References

1 John 3:14-18	Psalm 46:10
1 John 4:7,8	Isaiah 50:4,5
James 4:8	Psalm 51
Daniel 11:32	John 17
Psalm 122:6	Revelation 7:9,10

"The time will come when countless myriads will find music in the songs of Zion and solace in the parables of Galilee."

BENJAMIN DISRAELI (1804-1881)

PRIME MINISTER OF GREAT BRITAIN

Except the Lord build the house, they labour in vain that build it: except the Lord keep the city, the watchman waketh *but* in vain.

It is vain for you to rise up early, to sit up late, to eat the bread of sorrows: *for* so he giveth his beloved sleep.

Lo, children *are* an heritage of the Lord: *and* the fruit of the womb *is his* reward.

As arrows *are* in the hand of a mighty man; so *are* children of the youth.

Happy *is* the man that hath his quiver full of them: they shall not be ashamed, but they shall speak with the enemies in the gate.

PSALM 127:1-5

Celebration

Note

This mountain includes the arts, sports, entertainment, fashion, music, and other ways we enjoy life.

Prayer

Father, Your Word tells us that every good and perfect gift comes down from the Father of light. From the beginning to the end of the Bible You show Yourself as an awesome Creator. You love beauty, and the entire universe reflects this. The mountains and hills sing forth Your praise. Your creation causes us to praise You and the wonders of Your works in the earth.

In the name of Jesus we ask that in every area of entertainment an influence of Your righteousness will increase. We ask for an outpouring of Your gifts upon those in these different arenas, and that their talents will glorify You. Christians in the field of music, fashion, arts, sports, and entertainment will release songs and plays and works of art that display Your kingdom. Give them boldness in their creativity to share from the perspective of heaven. Let the works released by these Christians cause a new renaissance of the Holy Spirit in the marketplace.

The forces of darkness that would attempt to silence a moral voice in each of these arenas will not prevail against the kingdom of God. We stand against the spirit seeking to control music that influences our youth to go down paths of self-destruction. We say that the awesome presence of God will be like thunder and lightning revealing new songs that create a hunger to know the Lord.

Lord, release glory and shatter the darkness! May Your light infuse the spirits of our people with revelation of who You are. We pray Christian artists will spend more time in worship and will teach the songs that come out of these intimate times of worship. We break dullness of hearing off the ears of this generation of musicians and songwriters, so they will hear the sounds of heaven and release them in the earth. We desire for the song of the Lord to increase in every congregation and group of believers gathered to worship You.

In the name of Jesus we call for a revolution in the sports arena. We pray that athletes who serve You will have increased opportunities to share their testimony with other players and before the media. May all of the organizations that support Christian athletes experience a new wave of Your presence and provision so they can continue to minister to each generation gifted with physical abilities. Raise up bold servants in this area of entertainment, who celebrate the gifts given to them before the world. Increase the number of coaches who serve You and are not ashamed to live a holy life before the eyes of society.

Father, we pray the creativity You released to the builders of the Temple in Jerusalem be released again to those in the fashion industry. Our young people are drawn by the latest fads, and we need designers to create clothing with a kingdom-inspired message. Give them an open door to display their ideas in the marketplace. In the name of Jesus give them access to doors of opportunity and supernatural alignment. Provide finances and scholarships for study with teachers who can help strengthen their skills. Open doors of favor and make every crooked place straight so they can move into their destiny. Let their designs speak life and not darkness and death.

In the name of Jesus we ask for a revolution in the arts. We pray for filmmakers and artists and directors and actors who have Your heart. We say that the enemy of light will be pushed back as plays and movies are released that have a moral base and celebrate positive relationships. We pray for painters, sculptors, architects, and decorators to release works inspired by the Holy Spirit, like the cathedrals of old point the viewer toward God and creation.

Father, we thank You for all the gifts and talents that are in Your people. We speak life over any that are lying dormant. We ask for an explosion of supernatural creativity that will challenge our world to think once more that You are God and beside You there is no other, for the earth is Yours and the fullness thereof.

In the name of Jesus we pray. Amen.

Scripture References

James 1:17	Matthew 16:18
Genesis 1:1	Exodus 31:1-11
Isaiah 55:12	Isaiah 44:6-8
Psalm 19:1-6	Psalm 24:1

Family

Lord, we ask You to fill family leaders with the knowledge of Your will through all spiritual wisdom and understanding. This is so they can live in a manner that is worthy of You and may please You in every good work. We decree they trust in You, Lord, with all their heart, never relying on what they think they know. Lord, cause them to remember You in everything they do, and You will show them the right way. Open their eyes of understanding so they will know that marriage is not an institution but a relationship, and there's nothing more important than their relationship with You and one another.

We declare and decree that family leaders wait patiently before You and seek Your face. As they worship You, Lord, in spirit and truth, this creates a lifestyle of a heart of worship for them and their families. Thank You, Lord, for causing them to abide in a peaceful habitation, in secure dwellings, and in quiet resting places so that they lead their families out of the wellspring of full and whole spirits.

Thank You that family leaders are the gatekeepers of their families. The eyes of their hearts are enlightened in order that they may know the hope to which You have called them and their families. Give them the Issachar anointing so that they can understand the times and seasons for what their families should do. May they recognize the spiritual authority they have been given to demolish every demonic force set to bring chaos into their families. Thank You, Lord, that they possess the gates of their enemies.

May these leaders speak words from an instructed tongue, which gives life and hope to the weary. Give them the desire to guard their lips from all defilement. Give them words of truth and clarifying power. Lord, cause their words to affirm the vision You have for their families. May their words be so anointed with wisdom and reverence of You, Lord, that they turn their families from sin.

Lord, cause family leaders to accept the responsibility of being in positions of influence. May they be life-giving leaders who teach their families to love the Word of God, those who lead their families to meditate on the Word of God. Pour out Your anointing of wisdom so life-giving influence may flow out from them like a river. May they be life-giving leaders who bless the next generation with life-giving mentoring.

May our family leaders' lives be evident of love that is patient and kind, that does not envy, does not boast, and is not proud; love that is not rude, not self-seeking, is not easily angered, and keeps no record of wrongs; love that doesn't delight in evil but rejoices with the truth; love that always protects, always trusts, always hopes, always perseveres, and never fails. We ask You, Lord, to cause family leaders to keep before them faith, hope, love, and the remembrance that the greatest of these is love.

By Jacquelyn Marshall
Bible Teacher and Prayer Team Member—
Word Ministries
Written for *Prayers That Avail Much for Leaders*

Scriptures References

Colossians 1:9,10

Psalm 40:1

Isaiah 32:18

1 Chronicles 12:32

Isaiah 50:4

Proverbs 3:5,6

John 4:23

Ephesians 1:18

Genesis 24:60

1 Corinthians 13:4-7,13

APPENDIX A

Prayer to Receive Jesus as Your Lord and Savior

Father, it is written in Your Word that if I confess with my mouth that Jesus is Lord and believe in my heart that You have raised Him from the dead, I shall be saved. Therefore, Father, I confess that Jesus is my Lord. I make Him Lord of my life right now. I believe in my heart that You raised Jesus from the dead. I renounce my past life with Satan and close the door to any of his devices.

I thank You for forgiving me of all my sin. Jesus is my Lord, and I am a new creation. Old things have passed away; now all things become new in Jesus' name. Amen.

Scripture References

John 3:16	John 14:6
John 6:37	Romans 10:9,10
John 10:10	Romans 10:13
Romans 3:23	Ephesians 2:1-10
2 Corinthians 5:19	2 Corinthians 5:17
John 16:8,9	John 1:12
Romans 5:8	2 Corinthians 5:21

If you prayed the prayer to receive Jesus as Savior and
Lord for the first time, please contact us on the Web at
www.harrisonhouse.com to receive a free book.

Or you may write to us at

Harrison House
P.O. Box 35035
Tulsa, Oklahoma 74153

APPENDIX B

Prayer to Receive the Infilling of the Holy Spirit

My Heavenly Father, I am Your child, for I believe in my heart that Jesus has been raised from the dead, and I have confessed Him as my Lord.

Jesus said, "How much more shall your Heavenly Father give the Holy Spirit to those who ask Him." I ask You now in the name of Jesus to fill me with the Holy Spirit. I step into the fullness and power that I desire in the name of Jesus. I confess that I am a Spirit-filled Christian. As I yield my vocal organs by faith to You, my Lord, I expect to speak in tongues, for the Spirit gives me utterance in the name of Jesus. Praise the Lord! Amen.

Scripture References

John 14:16,17	Acts 19:2,5,6
Luke 11:13	Romans 10:9,10
Acts 1:8	1 Corinthians14:2-15
Acts 2:4	1 Corinthians 14:18,27
Acts 2:32,33,39	Ephesians 6:18
Acts 8:12-17	Jude 1:20
Acts 10:44-46	

APPENDIX C

Be Thou My Vision

Be Thou my Vision, O Lord of my heart;
Naught be all else to me, save that Thou art.
Thou my best Thought, by day or by night,
Waking or sleeping, Thy presence my light.
Be Thou my Wisdom, and Thou my true Word;
I ever with Thee and Thou with me, Lord;
Thou my great Father, I Thy true son;
Thou in me dwelling, and I with Thee one.
Be Thou my battle Shield, Sword for the fight;
Be Thou my Dignity, Thou my Delight;
Thou my soul's Shelter, Thou my high Tower:
Raise Thou me heavenward, O Power of my power.
Riches I heed not, nor man's empty praise,
Thou mine Inheritance, now and always:
Thou and Thou only, first in my heart,
High King of Heaven, my Treasure Thou art.
High King of Heaven, my victory won,
May I reach Heaven's joys, O bright Heaven's Sun!
Heart of my own heart, whatever befall,
Still be my Vision, O Ruler of all.

Words: Attributed to Dallan Forgaill, 8th Century (Rob
tu mo bhoile, a Comdi cride); translated from ancient Irish
to English by Mary E. Byrne, in "Eriú," Journal of the

School of Irish Learning, 1905, and versed by Eleanor H. Hull, 1912, alt.

Music: Slane, of Irish folk origin (MIDI, score). Slane Hill is about ten miles from Tara in County Meath. It was on Slane Hill around 433 AD that St. Patrick defied a royal edict by lighting candles on Easter Eve. High King Logaire of Tara had decreed that no one could light a fire before Logaire began the pagan spring festival by lighting a fire on Tara Hill. Logaire was so impressed by Patrick's devotion that, despite his defiance (or perhaps because of it), he let him continue his missionary work. The rest is history.

http://www.cyberhymnal.org

APPENDIX D

Darrell Scott Speaks to Congress

Darrell Scott, father of two Columbine High School victims of a shooting rampage conducted by two other students, spoke to Congress on May 27, 1999. Mr. Scott lost his daughter, and his son is recovering from the trauma of the event.

(Transcription courtesy NRA Members' Council of Contra Costa County)

At this very moment in a cemetery in southern Denver—Chapel Hill Cemetery—they're erecting thirteen crosses that I think are well known across the country, as a permanent memorial at the head of my daughter's grave. And my heart really longs to be there with my children, Bethany and her husband Don, Dana, Craig, and Mike, but it's with their blessing that I'm here today, and I appreciate that.

I realize that I'm a mere pawn in today's hearings, but I'm a willing pawn, because I dare to believe that I can make a difference. Every once in a while, a pawn has been used to checkmate a king. I have no hidden agenda, and of course I have no political aspirations. I simply speak to you as a brokenhearted father, and I only ask that you allow your heart to hear me for the next few minutes.

Since the dawn of creation, there has been both good and evil in the hearts of men and women, and we all contain those seeds. We contain the seeds of kindness and we contain the seeds of violence. And the death of my wonderful daughter, Rachel Joyce Scott, and the deaths of that heroic teacher, and the other eleven children who died, must not be in vain. Their blood cries out for answers.

The first recorded act of violence was when Cain slew his brother Abel out in the field. The villain was not the club he used, neither was it the NCA—the National Club Association—the true killer was Cain, and the reason for the murder could only be found in his heart. In the days that followed the Columbine tragedy, I was amazed at how quickly fingers began to be pointed at groups such as the NRA. I am not a member of the NRA. I am not a hunter. I do not even own a gun.

I'm not here to represent or to defend the NRA because I don't believe they are responsible for my daughter's death. Therefore, I don't believe they need to be defended by me. If I believed that they had anything to do with Rachel's murder, I would be their strongest opponent. I am here today to declare that Columbine was not just a tragedy, it was a spiritual event which should be forcing us to look at where the real blame lies. Much of that blame lies here in this room—much of that blame lies behind the pointing fingers of the accusers themselves.

I wrote a poem just four nights ago that expressed my feelings best, and it was written before I knew that I would be speaking here today, and I'd like to read that:

Your law's ignore our deepest needs.
Your words are empty air.
You've stripped away our heritage.
You've outlawed simple prayer.

Now' gunshots fill our classrooms.
And precious children die.
You seek for answers everywhere.
And ask the question "Why?"

You regulate restrictive laws.
Through legislative creed.
And yet you fail to understand.
That God is what we need.

— Darrell Scott

Men and women are three-part beings: we have a
body, and we have a soul, and we have a spirit…. And I
believe we fail to recognize that third element, that really
does need to be recognized by the legislative bodies of this
country, that's been ignored for so long. Spiritual influences were present within our educational systems for
most of our nation's history. Many of our major colleges
began as theological seminaries, and we know this is a
historic fact.

What has happened to us as a nation? We've refused
to honor God, and in doing so we opened the doors to
hatred and violence. And when something as terrible as
Columbine's tragedy occurs, politicians immediately look
for a scapegoat such as the NRA. They immediately seek
to pass more restrictive laws that continue to erode away
our personal and private liberties.

We don't need more restrictive laws. Erik and Dylan would not have been stopped by more gun laws or metal detectors. No amount of laws can stop someone who spends months of planning this type of massacre. The real villain lies within our own hearts. Political posturing and restrictive legislation are not the answers. The young people of our nation hold the key, and there is a spiritual awakening that is taking place that will not be squelched.

We don't need more religion. We don't need more gaudy television evangelists spewing out verbal religious garbage. We do not need more million-dollar church buildings built while people's basic needs are being ignored. We do need a change of heart and a humble acknowledgement that this nation was founded on the principle of simple trust in God.

When my son Craig lay under that table in the school library and saw his two friends murdered before his very eyes, he didn't hesitate to pray in school, and I defy any law or politician to deny him that right. I challenge every young person in America and around the world to realize that on April 20, 1999, at Columbine High School, prayer was brought back to our schools. Don't let the many prayers offered by those students be in vain. Dare to move into the new millennium with a sacred disregard for legislation that violates your conscience and denies your God-given right to communicate with Him.

And to those of you who would blame the NRA, I give to you a sincere challenge: dare to examine your own heart before you cast the first stone. My daughter's death will not be in vain. The young people of this country will not allow that to happen. And remember that even a pawn in a master's hand can accomplish much.

Thank you very much.

About the Authors

Germaine Griffin Copeland, founder and president of Word Ministries, Inc., organized in 1977, is the bestselling author of the *Prayers That Avail Much*® family of books. Her writings provide scriptural prayer and instruction to help you pray effectively for those things that concern you and your family and for other prayer assignments.

Germaine is the daughter of the late Reverend A. H. "Buck" Griffin, who served the Church of God (Cleveland, Tennessee) as a bishop for over forty years, and Donnis Brock Griffin, Bible teacher and exhorter. She and her husband, Everette, have four children and eleven grandchildren. Their prayer assignments increase as great-grandchildren are born into the family. Germaine and Everette reside in Greensboro, Georgia.

Lane M. Holland, MSN, M.Div., was born in Atlanta, Georgia, accepted Christ as her Savior at the age of five, and has followed Him ever since. She is an ordained minister of the Gospel of Jesus Christ and currently serves as pastor of a developing and dynamic church that was planted by her senior pastor several years ago in Tucker, Georgia. She is also the founder of Caring in the Name of Christ Ministries, which conducts conferences, training sessions, and a yearly prayer encounter for women each fall.

Lane's ministry has taken her throughout the United States and, since the early eighties, to many countries around the world. She has preached and taught in conferences, crusades, and Bible schools in South Korea, Thailand, Hong Kong, the Philippines, Indonesia, Malaysia, Nigeria, Sierra Leone, Zimbabwe, Morocco, Argentina, and other nations.

Lane is a gifted teacher of the Word of God. She seeks continually to understand the move of the Holy Spirit and is sensitive to His leading. Her call to preach came at sixteen years of age while serving in the youth ministry of her church, and she continues to serve as an Elder in her home church.

Lane received her B.A. in Psychology from Oglethorpe University in 1974. She received her Masters in Nursing, her R.N., and passed certification exams to receive her license as a Certified Nurse-Midwife from Yale University in 1980. She received her Masters of Divinity Degree from The McAfee School of Theology at Mercer University in Atlanta in 2006.

Lane has worked in both the public and private sectors in women's health care. She was an assistant professor at Yale University School of Nursing from 1981-1988. After returning to Atlanta she worked with a local obstetrician, and they established a private practice in the suburbs of Atlanta. She has received numerous honors and awards for academic achievement. She has also been published in health care journals and textbooks.

Lane finds her joy in worshiping the Lord and sharing the love of God with others all over the globe. Her primary focus is two-fold: global ministry and reminding the church of the power of prayer. She is the daughter of Lois Holland and the late Rufus Holland.

MISSION STATEMENT
WORD MINISTRIES, INC.

Motivating individuals to pray,

Encouraging them to achieve intimacy with God,

Bringing emotional wholeness and spiritual growth.

You may contact Word Ministries by writing:

Word Ministries, Inc.
Post Office Box 289
Good Hope, Georgia 30641

770.267.7603

www.prayers.org

Please include your testimonies and
praise reports when you write.

A TREASURY OF PRAYERS

Over 4 Million Sold in the Series!

Germaine Copeland's three bestselling volumes of *Prayers That Avail Much* have helped Christians learn how to pray, know what to pray, and confidently claim answers to prayer for more than twenty-five years. Now this all-in-one edition has been revised and expanded!

- An extensive scripture reference section!

- Beautiful, new text format

- And a special word from Germaine Copeland

This special clothbound edition is a treasured keepsake that will last for years to come, giving you the scripture-based prayers you know and trust for all of your life situations, plus every scripture reference right at your fingertips—a perfect gift for friends, loved ones, or yourself!

Prayers That Avail Much®, 25th Anniversary Commemorative Gift Edition

6" x 9" clothbound, 978-1-57794-752-3

Available at fine bookstores everywhere or visit www.harrisonhouse.com.

POWERFUL PRAYERS IN BEAUTIFUL LEATHER GIFT EDITIONS!

Now you can receive all three versions of Germaine Copeland's bestselling volumes of *Prayers That Avail Much* in a beautiful bonded leather gift edition celebrating 25 years! This anniversary edition includes an expanded scripture reference section at the back for easy reference to every scripture used to formulate Germaine's powerful prayers.

A wonderful gift for those just beginning their prayer life and for seasoned prayer warriors, this slim, flexible, bonded leather edition with a ribbon marker is great for those on the go. It's a perfect companion for devotional Bible study and for corporate prayer.

Prayers That Avail Much®, 25th Anniversary Leather Gift Edition

4 ⁵/₈" x 7" bonded leather with presentation box

Burgundy, 978-1-57794-753-0

Navy, 978-1-57794-754-7

PRAYERS THAT AVAIL MUCH
COMMEMORATIVE EDITION AUDIO BOOK

Germaine Copeland's three bestselling volumes of *Prayers That Avail Much* have helped Christians learn how to pray, know what to pray, and confidently claim answers to prayer for more than twenty-five years. Now this all-in-one edition of scripture-based prayers is available as an audio book! Listen and pray with these powerful prayers in this unabridged, complete collection.

Prayers That Avail Much Commemorative Edition Audio Book

9 CDs, 978-1-57794-999-4

Available at fine bookstores everywhere or visit www.harrisonhouse.com.

POCKET EDITIONS FOR BUSY LIFESTYLES!

For those on the go, *Prayers That Avail Much* pocket editions make great gifts for just about anyone! These compact-sized books with shortened scriptural prayers are perfect for beach bags or briefcases. Take the power of God's Word into every situation!

Prayers That Avail Much for Moms (pocket edition)
4" x 6" paperback • 978-1-57794-641-0

Prayers That Avail Much for Women (pocket edition)
4" x 6" paperback • 978-1-57794-642-7

Prayers That Avail Much for Men (pocket edition)
4" x 6" paperback • 978-1-57794-643-4

Available at fine bookstore everywhere
or visit www.harrisonhouse.com.

Fast. Easy.
Convenient.

For the latest Harrison House product information and author news, look no further than your computer. All the details on our powerful, life-changing products are just a click away. New releases, E-mail subscriptions, Podcasts, testimonies, monthly specials—find it all in one place. Visit harrisonhouse.com today!

harrisonhouse

THE HARRISON HOUSE VISION

Proclaiming the truth and the power
Of the Gospel of Jesus Christ
With excellence;

Challenging Christians to
Live victoriously,
Grow spiritually,
Know God intimately.